Indian Army Aviation 2025

Indian Army Aviation 2025

Edited by
Lt. Gen. Vijay Oberoi, PVSM, AVSM
and Col. Utkarsh S. Rathore

Centre for Land Warfare Studies
New Delhi

in association with

KNOWLEDGE WORLD

KW Publishers Pvt Ltd
New Delhi

KNOWLEDGE WORLD

KW Publishers Book
www.kwpublishers.com

Published in India by

Kalpana Shukla
KW Publishers Pvt Ltd
5A/4A, Ansari Road, Daryaganj, New Delhi 110002
email: knowledgeworld@vsnl.net / online.kw@gmail.com

ISBN: 978-81-87966-63-0

Transcribed and Compiled by Col. Utkarsh S. Rathore, Deputy Director, Centre for Land Warfare Studies.

Typeset by Dharana, New Delhi; studiodharana@gmail.com
Printed at Chaman Offset Printer, New Delhi

Centre for Land Warfare Studies (CLAWS)

CLAWS was established in December 2003, as an independent think-tank, devoted to the promotion and furtherance of intellectual pursuit in the art, science and literature of land warfare. The vision of the centre is to be a pioneer in futuristic thinking about all aspects of land warfare, as they relate to operations within the region.

The centre hopes to attract leading strategic thinkers, defence analysts and academicians to deliberate over every facet of land warfare, from the minuscule to the mega, so that it can be disseminated to the professionals of the armed forces, as well as to all citizens of our nation. The effort would be to develop strategic culture in general and professional nuances in particular, so that the armed forces and the political leadership, on the one hand; and the academia, the intellectuals and the person on the street, on the other, benefit from it.

In 2005, CLAWS had organised two seminars in New Delhi and Pune. This book contains the proceedings of the two seminars, as well as the papers presented during the various sessions.

Contents

Contributors

Brigadier Gurmeet Kanwal

Brigadier Gurmeet Kanwal commanded an infantry brigade in high-altitude on the line of control (LoC) with Pakistan during Operation Parakaram and an artillery field regiment in counter-insurgency (CI) operations in the Kashmir Valley during Operation Rakshak. He has served at Headquarters Integrated Defence Staff (IDS), Directorate General of Military Operations (DGMO) at Army Headquarters, United Nations Military Observer Group (UNTAG) in Namibia, as a brigade major of an infantry brigade and as an instructor of gunnery at the School of Artillery.

A former senior fellow at the Institute for Defence Studies and Analyses (IDSA), New Delhi, Brigadier Kanwal has authored several books including 'Nuclear Defence: Shaping the Arsenal'; 'Pakistan s Proxy War'; 'Heroes of Kargil'; 'Kargil '99: Blood, Guts and Firepower'; and 'Artillery: Honour and Glory'. He has contributed extensively to Strategic Analysis, Indian Defence Review and other military journals of repute, as well as leading national newspapers. He wrote a regular column on national security for The Statesman for over two years. He is also a keen photographer and has published a large number of photographs.

He opted for voluntary retirement to take up writing and strategic analysis full time. He is currently Senior Fellow, Centre for Air Power Studies, New Delhi.

Rear Admiral K. Raja Menon

Admiral Menon was a career officer and a submarine specialist in the Indian Navy. He commanded seven ships and submarines. He retired in 1994 as the Assistant Chief of Naval Staff (Operations). He has participated in military confidence-building measures talks with neighbouring countries and was in the first military delegation to Pakistan. After retiring he authored three books, '*Maritime Strategy and Continental Wars*', which is a standard text in the Navy and led to extensive consultant work with the IDS and Naval Headquarters. His second book, '*A Nuclear Strategy for India*' has been well received in India and abroad. His third book, '*The Indian Navy: A Photo Essay*' is the official gift of the

Navy. An edited book, '*Weapons of Mass Destruction: Options for India*' has been released by Sage India and is receiving press reviews currently. An occasional paper of his, titled 'The US-India Non-proliferation Divide; the Way Ahead' was published in the USA by Co-operative Monitoring Centre, Sandia in 2005.

Admiral Menon was a member of the Arun Singh Committee to restructure the national defence set up in India, and a member of the National Defence University Committee. He is a visiting lecturer at all institutes of higher study of the Indian armed forces and organised the first Nuclear Management Course for Indian service officers. He headed the Defence Research and Development Organisation (DRDO) funded study on 'Pakistan Ballistic Missiles and their effect on Indian National Security'. He is currently head of a group engaged in writing the Indian Naval Maritime Strategy. He is also the Chairman of the Task Force on Net Assessment and Simulation in the National Security Council. He writes for the Outlook and the Indian Express and is engaged in many Track II initiatives with Pakistan and China having travelled extensively in both countries.

Lieutenant General Amitava Mukherjee, PVSM, AVSM

Lieutenant General Mukherjee was commissioned into the Regiment of Artillery in June 1960. After his initial service in the field branch of artillery he sidestepped to Air Defence Artillery and commanded a Schilka Regiment, a Kavadrat Missile Group and an Air Defence Brigade. He has done two foreign courses on Schilka Air Defence Weapon Systems and Operational Logistics in the erstwhile Soviet Union.

General Mukherjee has a rich and varied instructional and staff experience at various levels and has seen active combat service in 1962, 1965 and 1971. Before his superannuation in February 2001, he was Director General Army Air Defence for four years during the critical period when it had bifurcated from its parent arm -the Regiment of Artillery.

Lieutenant General Vijay Oberoi, PVSM, AVSM, VSM

Lieutenant General Vijay Oberoi was commissioned in the Maratha Light Infantry in 1961. A graduate of the Defence Services Staff College (DSSC), he later did his MSc in defence studies from Madras University. He was an International Fellow at the United States Army War College in USA in 1988-89. He has held a number of prestigious staff and instructional appointments, including the appointment of Defence Adviser at Kuala Lumpur (Malaysia), during his army service.

The General has the rare distinction of commanding an armoured division, despite being an infantry officer. He had commanded a Strike Corps, and had also held the prestigious appointment of DGMO. He had the honour to be appointed the 'Colonel' of the Maratha Light Infantry Regiment, for a tenure of over eight years.

General Oberoi was severely wounded during the 1965 Indo-Pak conflict, wherein he lost his right leg. Despite his disability, he rose steadily in the army, till he retired as the Vice Chief of Army Staff (VCOAS) in September 2001. Prior to that, he had commanded two Armies- the Army Training Command (ARTRAC) at Shimla and the prestigious Western Command at Chandimandir.

After his retirement, he resides at Panchkula, and devotes considerable time in writing for newspapers and professional magazines, participating in seminars and panel discussions, and delivering lectures, mostly on security related issues and international relations.

In 2003, he set up the Centre for Land Warfare Studies (CLAWS), of which he is the Director. He is also the President of the War Wounded Foundation, set up to work towards meaningful rehabilitation of the war disabled.

Vice Admiral Vinod Pasricha

The Admiral was commissioned on July 1, 1963. He underwent flying training with the Indian Air Force (MF) and graduated as a naval fighter pilot on the Seahawk aircraft operating from INS Vikrant and later commanded the same squadron. He has also done an operational flying tenure with the IAF. As a regular naval officer he primarily held operational appointments. These included commands of a Petya class frigate -INS Katchall and of India's indigenous frigate -INS Vindhyagiri, and followed by being nominated as the commanding officer designate of India's second aircraft carrier -INS Viraat. For this he led a team in May 1986 to Plymouth UK, where the carrier was commissioned.

As a Rear Admiral, he has held assignments as the Assistant Chief of the Naval Staff (Air) at Naval Headquarters, Flag Officer Naval Aviation, Goa and the Flag Officer Commanding (FOC), Maharashtra Naval Area. On promotion to Vice Admiral, he took over as the Commandant of the National Defence College (NDC), New Delhi, followed by his appointment as the Deputy Chief of the Naval Staff, looking after naval operations. In February 1998, he took over as the Flag Officer Commanding-in-Chief (FOC-in-C) of the Eastern Naval Command based at Visakhapatnam. Then he moved as the FOC-in-C of the Western Naval Command. Thus, he attained the unique distinction of having held command of both the operational theatres of the Indian Navy.

Colonel U.S. Rathore

Colonel Utkarsh S. Rathore was commissioned in 1980 from the Officers' Training Academy, Chennai. He commanded 17th Battalion the Maratha Light Infantry in Operations Rakshak and Parakram. The Colonel has a rich service experience of high altitude and counter-insurgency environment. He has been an instructor in Senior Command Wing at Army War College, Mhow. Colonel Rathore is a founder member of the Centre for Land Warfare Studies.

Lieutenant General Vinay Shankar, PVSM, AVSM, VSM

Lieutenant General Vinay Shankar was commissioned into the Regiment of Artillery in June 1960. He took part in the wars of 1962, 1965 and 1971. He became an army aviator and flew for four years. He has served in the insurgency areas of Nagaland and Manipur.

He has attended the DSSC, Higher Command and the NDC courses.

The General was the Director General Artillery from January 1998 to December 2000 and was involved in the conduct of the Kargil operations in 1999. He retired in December 2000.

He has been a columnist with the Asian Age for over three years and has also contributed articles for other magazines and newspapers. He is also an editorial consultant to the Indian Defense Review and member of the executive council of the United Services Institution (USI) of India.

Lieutenant General G.S. Sihota, PVSM, AVSM, VrC, VM

Lieutenant General G.S. Sihota was commissioned into the Regiment of Artillery and awarded 'Silver Gun' for topping the Young Officer's Course. He is an Air Observation Post (Air OP) pilot and the recipient of the 'Silver Pushpak' for topping the basic course.

He has attended courses at DSSC, Camberley (UK); Chemical Officers Advance Course, Alabama (USA) and NDC, New Delhi.

He took part in Indo-Pak wars of 1965 and 1971 and was decorated with a Vir Chakra in 1971. He successfully converted an infantry brigade into a mechanised brigade. He also raised the CI Force 'Victor' in J&K.

The General has been DGMO and retired as General Officer Commanding-in-Chief (GOC-in-C) Southern Command, after a distinguished career spanning over 40 years.

Brigadier Devinder Singh, VSM

Brigadier Devinder Singh was commissioned into the Regiment of Artillery in 1970. He is a graduate of DSSC, Wellington and attended the Higher Command

Course at Army War College, Mhow. On becoming a Brigadier he was side-stepped to General Cadre.

He saw combat both during 1971 with the Parachute Brigade and during the 1999 Kargil War where he commanded an infantry brigade responsible for the eviction operations in Batalik Sector. He has extensive exposure in CI operations having commanded his unit in the Northeast and a brigade in Kashmir Valley apart from tenures with OFC HQ's in Sri Lanka, in Operation Blue Star and elsewhere. He has held numerous general staff and instructional appointments.

The Brigadier is a helicopter pilot having served with the Army Aviation Corps (AAC). He is also a paratrooper. He has also been Member Army and Senior Fellow at the IDSA, New Delhi. His specialised training, broad spectrum exposure and operational experience in command and other assignments have bestowed him a good grasp over military dimensions of India's security environment.

He is presently posted as Brigadier General Staff -Concepts in the Doctrine Branch at Headquarters ARTRAC, Shimla.

Air Commodore Jasjit Singh, AVSM, VrC, VM

Air Commodore Jasjit Singh, FAeSI and MA (Hist), is a former Director of Operations of IAF and is currently Director, Centre for Air Power Studies, New Delhi. He headed the IDSA, New Delhi (1987-2001). Author and contributor-editor of more than three dozen books including '*Air Power in Modem Warfare*' (1985); '*Non-provocative Defence*' (1989); '*Nuclear India*' (1998); '*India's Defence Spending*' (2001); '*Air Power and Joint Operations*' (2003); '*Iraq War*' (2004) and '*Nuclear Deterrence and Diplomacy*' (2004). He has published extensively on strategic and security issues. He was Convenor of the Task Force to set up National Security Council and member of the National Security Advisory Board. He is a member of the International Commission for Peace and a Fellow of World Academy of Arts and Science.

Acronyms and Abbreviations

ASW	Anti-Submarine Warfare
FEBA	Forward Edge of Battle Area
PAA	Pakistan Army Aviation
LICO	Low Intensity Conflict Operations
LIC	Low Intensity Conflict
SIGNIT	Signal Intelligence
ARI	Aviation Restructure Initiative
ROAD	Reorganised Objectives Army Division
TEWT	Tactical Exercise Without Troops
AAC	Army Aviation Corps
AAM	Air-to-Air Missile
AD	Air Defence
ADF	Australian Defence Forces
AGPL	Actual Ground Position Line
AHC	Assault Helicopter Company
ALG	Advance Landing Ground
ALH	Advanced Light Helicopter
AOE	Army of Excellence
AOP	Air Observation Post
ARTRAC	Army Training Command
ASM	Air-to-Surface Missile
ATC	Air Traffic Control
AWAC	Airborne Warning and Control
BAI	Battlefield Air Interdiction
BSS	Battlefield Surveillance System
C^3I	Command, Control, Communication and Intelligence
C^4ISR	Command, Control, Communications, Computers, Intelligence, Sensors and Reconnaissance
CAC	Command Aviation Company
Cas evac	Casualty Evacuation
CATS	Combat Army Aviation Training School
CDS	Chief of Defence Staff

CI	Counter-Insurgency
C-in-C	Commander-in-Chief
COAS	Chief of Army Staff
COTS	Commercially off the Shelf
CT	Counter-Terrorist, Counter-Terrorism
DGMO	Directorate General of Military Operations
DRDO	Defence Research and Development Organisation
DSSC	Defence Service Staff College
ECM	Electronic Countermeasure
ELINT	Electronic Intelligence
EME	Electrical and Mechanical Engineering
ESM	Electronic Support Measure
EW	Electronic Warfare
FAARP	Forward Arming and Replenishment Point
FAC	Forward Air Controller
FFAR	Fin Folding Aerial Rocket
FGA	Fighter Ground Attack
FLET	Forward Line of Enemy Troops
FLOT	Forward Line of Own Troops
FOFA	Follow on Forces Attack
FOO	Forward Observation Officer
GHQ	General Headquarters
GPS	Global Positioning System
GWOT	Global War on Terrorism
HAL	Hindustan Aeronautics Limited
Heliborne	Helicopter Borne
IAF	Indian Air Force, Israeli Air Force
IDF	Indian Defence Forces, Israeli Defence Forces
IDS	Integrated Defence Staff
IDSA	Institute of Defence Studies and Analysis
IFF	Identification Friend or Foe
IMINT	Imagery Intelligence
ISR	Intelligence, Surveillance and Reconnaissance
ISTAR	Integrated, Surveillance, Target Acquisition Radar
IT	Information Technology
IW	Information Warfare
JAAT	Joint Air Attack Team
JHC	Joint Helicopter Command
JSTARS	Joint-Surveillance and Target Attack Radar Systems
LAC	Line of Actual Control

LoC	Line of Control
LOROP	Long Range Oblique Photography
MR	Maritime Reconnaissance
MoD	Ministry of Defence
MR	Military Region
MTI	Moving Target Indication
NATO	North Atlantic Treaty Organisation
NBC	Nuclear, Biological and Chemical
NDC	National Defence College
NOE	Nap-of-the-earth
OOA	Out of Area
OOW	Operations Other Than War
PGM	Precision Guided Munition
PLA	People's Liberation Army
PLAAC	People's Liberation Army Aviation Corps
PLAAF	People's Liberation Army Air Force
POK	Pakistan Occupied Kashmir
R&O	Reconnaissance and Observation
RAAF	Royal Australian Air Force
RAF	Royal Air Force
RAS	Regimental Aviation Squadron
RFC	Royal Flying Corps
RMA	Revolution in Military Affairs
RSTA	Reconnaissance, Surveillance and Target Acquisition
SAM	Surface-to-Air Missile
SAR	Synthetic Aperture Radar
SAED	Suppression of Enemy Air Defence
SF	Special Forces
TAC	Tactical Air Centre
TADS	Target Acquisition Designation System
TBA	Tactical Battle Area
TBS	Tactical Battle Support
TI	Thermal Imaging
UAV	Unmanned Aerial Vehicle
USAAF	United States Army Air Force
USAF	United States Air Force
USI	United Service Institution
VCOAS	Vice Chief of Army Staff
WSI	Weapon Support Integrated

Foreword

The growth of Indian Army Aviation has been haphazard and by fits and starts. Although Army Aviation came into its own as an integral part of the Army in 1986, it continues to be plagued with many infirmities. Foremost amongst these is the opposition of the Indian Air Force (IAF), whenever the question of expansion of the role of Army Aviation comes up for discussion. Essentially, the opposition of the IAF relates to 'turf'. The IAF wants to continue to hold on to those assets that logically must come under the ambit of the Army. Their main argument is that centralized control results in better cost-effectiveness. This may be theoretically right, but it ignores the reality that no amount of coordination between the Army and the IAF can replace the kind of intimate and readily available support the Army needs in crucial areas during operations.

Today, Army Aviation has the largest number of helicopters amongst the three services. Despite this, it has very few helicopters to carry out a number of extremely specialised roles in the tactical battle area. It is only recently that it has commenced the intake of utility helicopters, but the numbers are nowhere near what the Army needs. The dependence of the Army on the IAF for even tactical movements continues to be near total. This results in avoidable delays, lack of understanding between the troops on the ground and the IAF pilots and missing important tactical opportunities. A similar situation prevails in the employment of attack helicopters, which continue to be with the IAF. India is perhaps the only important country in the world where such dichotomy exists. Attack helicopters are an integral part of the land battle, wherein mechanized forces fight the battle in concert with the attack helicopters. The type of integrated and intimate training required between the mechanized forces and the attack helicopters, to employ them in unison, is obviously not possible when the two entities are controlled by two different services.

The third area of dissonance is the many objections of the IAF to the induction of fixed wing aircraft in Army Aviation. The Army has legitimate requirements for small fixed wing aircraft, especially for important roles like command and control, aerial communication hubs, tactical lift within an army theatre, logistics including casualty evacuation, communication flights and so on. However, the IAF is adamant. This ostrich-like attitude makes little sense, especially when the Indian Navy, the Indian Coast Guard and even central police forces like the Border Security Force (BSF) and others already have fixed wing aircraft in their inventory.

A survey of military aviation organisations, within and outside the country reveals the inadequacies of our Army Aviation. It has braved the neglect of years and has performed creditably with its meager resources in multi-terrain and operational conditions, but unless it is rapidly modernized, it will not be able to keep up and support the field formations in the changing battlefields of the future.

Resistance from the IAF will persist, but the Army will have to take a firm and unambiguous stand by garnering support for its legitimate and logical demands. There should also be more public debates on the dire need for restructuring Army Aviation. Our political leadership also needs to step in. A good forum for discussion is the Standing Committee of Parliament for Defence.

Army Aviation assets are needed at all formations from command to divisional levels and in some cases to independent brigade group levels too. At present, Army Aviation assets are inadequate for the size of the Indian Army and the tasks it is required to perform. Even the current growth plan appears somewhat modest when the totality of requirements is worked out. The expansion of Army Aviation is therefore an imperative. Army Aviation should possess a mix of fixed wing aircraft, light / medium helicopters, duly modified for various roles like reconnaissance, surveillance, gunship, attack, command post and combat service support. In a later time-frame, heavy helicopters may also be considered for induction.

The operational diversities of the Indian Army, coupled with the variety of terrain, extensive deployment in mountainous and high altitude areas, need for over the crest line observation for reconnaissance by field commanders, direction of artillery fire, casualty evacuation from inaccessible areas and speedy move of commanders to the forward posts that are difficult to access, make the need for a dedicated aviation unit (reconnaissance and observation squadron) for every infantry and mountain division a necessity.

Mechanised warfare in plains and desert terrain requires the integration of the third dimension with mechanised forces, by way of attack and scout helicopters. All armoured divisions and RAPIDs need a dedicated attack helicopter squadron, in addition to a reconnaissance and observation squadron.

Headquarters command and corps should have aviation brigades' orbated to them. These brigades should be equipped to carry out reconnaissance, attack, support and mobility operations, in support of the command / corps or subordinate formations.

One or more composite squadrons, equipped with light and medium lift helicopters need to be urgently raised and fully integrated with our Special Forces. Depending on the roles and tasks, there may also be a need for surveillance and armed helicopters being grouped with these special composite squadrons.

At present, Unarmed Aerial Vehicles (UAV's) form part of the regiment of artillery. This was done when the erstwhile 'locating' units of artillery were reorganised into Surveillance and Target Acquisition (SATA) units, perhaps because of the surveillance function they performed. At that stage, no cognisance was taken of the expertise of army aviation. I am a strong advocate of re-allocating UAV's from artillery to army aviation. This would achieve optimum results and is a cost-effective option.

All logistics functions need to be integrated within Army Aviation and the present system of control of logistics manpower by different services needs to be dispensed with.

Army aviation needs to develop organizations that enhance aviation capabilities to support the concepts of operations of field commanders. The force structure should be tailored to meet evolving operational requirements. In addition, aviation organizations should include appropriate maintenance and logistical support elements required to sustain the force.

Army Aviation leadership development also needs to be expanded to prepare aviation leaders for the diverse challenges that this versatile force requires. The future aviator needs to imbibe technology, as well as acquire and master the skills necessary to win and survive on the battlefield of the future. Cadre management of Army Aviation needs attention, in order to raise a pilot cadre which is available for meeting the growth plans of the Corps.

We at CLAWS had selected the subject of Army Aviation for this detailed study, as in our perception there was inadequate knowledge of the state of Army Aviation, as well as its overwhelming importance on the modern battlefield. With a view to obtain views and opinions from large numbers, we had conducted two seminars on the subject. The first seminar was held at New Delhi and the second at Pune. The participants as well as the delegates who attended were different. We had also co-opted participants and delegates from all the three services, so that all possible views could be aired. This volume contains some of the papers presented and the entire proceedings of the two seminars. The views contained in this volume are those of the authors in their individual capacity and do not necessarily reflect the policy of any organization or institution.

I am sanguine that this volume will generate debate and discussion on this important subject. Besides whetting the appetite of professionals and analysts, I feel it would educate the lay reader in one more facet of the military, a facet which will increasingly become a force multiplier and a battle winning factor.

New Delhi
30 October 2007

Lt Gen Vijay Oberoi
Director

Inaugural Address

— **Lieutenant General B.S. Thakur, PVSM, AVSM, ADC**
Vice Chief of Army Staff

General Sharma, Vice Admiral Chopra, Lieutenant General Oberoi, ladies and gentlemen. It gives me great pleasure to be here this morning at this seminar on army aviation. I would like to congratulate the Centre for Land Warfare Studies for bringing together such a galaxy of professionals from all the three Services to deliberate upon this important subject.

I am particularly glad to see a large number of serving officers from all three services in the audience. I would urge them to listen and reflect on the views of various analysts with an open mind and derive full value from the presentations and the discussions.

The AAC of the Indian Army has now been in existence for nearly twenty years. Although, the need for the aviation corps had been felt much earlier. This youngest arm of the army has served with much distinction in last so many years and has earned for itself a reputation of a highly efficient and a professional force. The exploits of our aviators in wars and operations other than war (OOTW) are well known to this audience and I do not need to repeat them here.

Despite the highly professional manner in which the army aviation has functioned, it still lacks the wherewithal and structures for providing the complete ambit of support, which the army needs. We in the army are convinced that keeping in the view the wars and conflicts the army has to fight in future; the AAC has to grow substantially. The contours of this growth will no doubt be discussed during the seminar in the two sessions that have been planned. It is essential that during the discussions you look at army aviation in its totality, so that practical and workable recommendations emerge, which will then be assessed in in-house exercises for planning and executing the growth of AAC.

Before you commence your deliberations, it may be useful to take a broad look at the prevailing and future security environment so that your deliberations remain focused. We are in an era of change. The nature of war has also changed and in many respect it continues to change on account of environmental and situational factors. We are already in the era of 'fewer wars and more conflicts' and this is likely to be the norm in the future. Low intensity conflict operations (LICO), countering terrorism — both state sponsored and by non-state actors and similar sub-conventional operations have assumed much grater importance than hitherto fore.

All these changes and those in the offing have a direct impact on how the armies are going to carry out their tasks of deterrence and waging war. Although, non-military tasks are increasingly acquiring prominence in inter-state relations, military power as a factor in the overall power of states remains crucial.

India's strategic concerns are not confined to the subcontinent but encompass the entire Indian Ocean area, from the eastern seaboard of Africa in the west to the Malacca Straits in the east, that includes Afghanistan, Iran, Central Asian Republics (CARs), China, Myanmar and the littoral countries of Southeast Asia. India aspires to be recognised as an economic and military power of some reckoning; this entails, among other facets, the capability to project power in the region, when our interests so demand. Such an aspiration requires modern armed forces, while ensuring sustained economic growth and development.

India's military strategy needs to be effective across the entire spectrum of conflict — from a high intensity conventional war, under the backdrop of a nuclear threat, to a low intensity conflict (LIC), which may include high-intensity insurgency, militancy and terrorism. Military contingencies will increasingly require multi-faceted forces with skills to handle both combat and non-traditional situations. This is because the security challenges will be more ambiguous and will follow less traditional paths in the future.

Army aviation will increasingly become more relevant in all types of operations in the future. The Indian Army has to maintain a high-level of readiness for war in varied terrain conditions and should have the capability to operate in the complete spectrum of conflict. Army aviation is an important and integral part of a modern army and hence its structures, manpower, equipment, doctrine and concepts of employment also need to be contemporary and must keep pace with modern armies.

The operations of army aviation will greatly assist the field force in achieving its military objectives. Army aviation is a force multiplier on account of its ability to quickly engage, disengage and regroup in the battle zone. It gives additional tactical capability to the field commanders as their area of influence increases.

Army aviation enables them, in counter insurgency operations, wherein, its tasks include detection by sensors, raids by armed helicopters, movement of reinforcements by utility helicopters.

These is a broad consensus in the army that army aviation needs to play a vastly enhanced role in land operations in the coming years. This is only possible if the army aviation grows, both qualitatively and quantitatively.

Today the army aviation does field the largest force of light helicopters amongst the three services. But the scenario is quite different in other areas. As an example, even the attack helicopters, though under the nominal command of the army, are in fact manned, controlled and owned by the air force. We need an air arm which can meet the diverse needs of the field commanders in various types of operations, where intimate and readily available support is a must.

For dominating the tactical battle space of the 21st century, the army must go beyond just fielding the light observation helicopters and a few utility helicopters and using attack helicopters by proxy. The need is to create a dedicated and fully capable aviation corps. There is a need to carry out an in-depth study regarding the roles, which the army aviation needs to play, its organisations, structures, command and control, equipment, manpower, selection and training, as well as the manner in which this extremely important arm of the army will function in both peace and war. This needs to be in the context of the likely threats to the nation, how they are sought to be tackled, the changing nature of war and conflicts and the impact of technology.

I am sanguine that all the aspects will engage your attention during the seminar. I will suggest that you make your discussion as broad-based as possible, so that preconceived notions are not allowed to obscure the aim of the seminar, which is to look at army aviation in a holistic manner and suggest changes, which are not only in tune with the global norms and the changing security environment but which also take in to account special conditions which obtain in our country and our region. I have no doubt that by the end of the day a coherent picture will emerge regarding the direction we need to take to make the army aviation a formidable and potent arm of the Indian Army. ■

Approach Paper

Optimisation of Indian Army Aviation—An Approach

— **Lieutenant General Vijay Oberoi**

Introduction

The advent of air power in the 20th century revolutionised warfare by adding a third dimension to the battlefield on land and at sea. In the beginning, air elements employed by the military were part of the army. However, gradually air forces emerged as separate services, keeping in view their roles and the tasks they were performing. This separation from the army was faster in some countries, while in others it was achieved after much greater deliberations. The emergence of the US Air Force (USAF), as a separate service is a good example.

It was soon realised by both the army and the navy that there were many tasks which could be best performed only by integral aviation resources. This was despite the fact that air forces were tasked to provide air support for the other two services in many situations, and detailed procedures were formulated jointly for such support. Conflicts in various parts of the world further reinforced the need for integral aviation resources which would provide the field force commander real-time battlefield flexibility and consequent enhancement in combat power. The third dimension soon became an essential part of the planning ambit of the field commander.

In some countries, the advent of army aviation was a smooth process, but in others, the air forces concerned opposed it in varying degrees. Their reasoning was that it was a wasteful process, as the air forces were, in any case, tasked to provide all types of support to the ground forces. They also argued that all air components must be centrally controlled for optimum functioning and best results. The view of the ground forces on the other hand, was that while the roles and tasks were quite clear, optimum results in certain specific areas and functions could only be obtained when air assets meant to perform such functions were directly controlled by the field commanders of the army, and hence had to be part of army formations at successive levels.

India was perhaps one of the few countries fielding a highly professional and large army, where the air force clung to what it considered its legitimate turf for a very long time. The proposal for an aviation corps for the army was first mooted in 1963 by the then Chief of Army Staff (COAS) General J.N. Chaudhury, but it was only in 1986 that it saw the light of the day, after considerable opposition and great reluctance from the IAF. Even today, the aviation arm of the Indian Army lacks the wherewithal to be a full-fledged AAC.

Indian Army Aviation Corps

There are two events of importance in the history of army aviation in India. These are the raising of the first Air OP Squadron in 1942 and the creation of AAC in 1986. Despite their limitations, the Air OP units of yore performed creditably and their pilots were the pioneers of the AAC.

Efforts for the creation of an AAC are too numerous to be mentioned here, except to highlight that there was considerable debate and innumerable discussions leading to the birth of the AAC on November 1, 1986. The salient points of the decision to create the AAC were as under:-

- All Air OP units to be transferred to the army, and to be wholly manned, maintained and controlled by it.
- Army to have its own utility helicopter units, which will be wholly manned, maintained and controlled by it.
- Attack helicopter units will continue to be air force assets, but will be placed under the command and control of the army.
- Army will create its own Air Traffic Control (ATC) facilities at army aviation bases.
- Army will create its own organisational infrastructure for the management of its army aviation units.

At present, army aviation has 11 squadrons organised in 34 light reconnaissance and observation (R&O) flights, equipped with a total of 180 Chetak and Cheetah helicopters of 1960 and 1970 vintages, as well as two utility squadrons equipped with the Advanced Light Helicopter (ALH). Although army aviation became an integral arm of the army nearly 20 years back, its growth has been tardy and not in tune with the vision when it was raised. In 1986, it had eight squadrons. It took 13 years to raise the strength to 11 squadrons, where it continues till today.

The AAC currently flies 180 helicopters, consisting of 60 Chetaks (Alouette II) and 120 Cheetahs (Alouette III). The 80 newest Cheetah airframes were marginally upgraded to the Lancer configuration, at the rate of four per month, commencing 2002. The Chetaks are organised into six squadrons, which are assigned to corps headquarters. The Cheetahs and Lancers are organised into six-squadron establishments, which support independent flights of five helicopters each and are attached to divisional headquarters. The AAC currently has approximately 460 officer pilots on strength and an annual intake of 40-45 officers. The AAC Centre is at Nasik (Maharashtra). Army aviation training, which was previously carried out at the School of Artillery at Deolali (Maharashtra), is now carried out at an independent Combat Air Training School (CATS), also at Deolali.

Army aviation needs to perform a variety of roles, to be called a complete force, but the present structure of the AAC inhibits it from performing all roles it should perform. The roles it must perform are attack, combat fire support, surveillance - both electronic and visual, as well as aerial photography; tactical lift, provision of airborne command posts, electronic warfare (EW), monitoring of the nuclear, biological and chemical (NBC) environment; logistical functions; communications and casualty evacuation (cas evac).

Army aviation is a force multiplier on account of its ability to quickly engage, disengage and regroup in the battle zone. It gives additional tactical capabilities to the field commanders, as their areas of influence increases. Army aviation enables them to exploit fleeting opportunities. Army aviation plays an important role in CI operations too. It includes detection by sensors, raids by armed helicopters, and movement of reinforcements speedily by utility helicopters.

The size of the AAC is puny by most parameters. It has been unable to grow to its natural size on account of a number of factors, which include, opposition from the air force, insufficient interest by the army hierarchy, a lack of vision and financial constraints. Consequently, the AAC, as presently structured, has a number of limitations; some of these are:-

- Lack of modern helicopters with all-weather capabilities.
- Minuscule tactical lift capability.
- Absence of weapon platforms.
- Limited night-flying and no night-fighting capability.
- Absence of electronic surveillance devices.
- No capability for passage of real-time information.

With a view to streamline it's functioning and overcome the limitations, a growth plan has been formulated, which envisages an accretion of more than 300 modern aircraft, in addition to the upgradation/ replacement of the existing fleet. Salient features of this plan are enumerated in succeeding paragraphs.

Accretion Plan-2017 envisages a full complement fleet comprising attack, utility and light helicopters, as well as fixed-wing aircraft for communications, logistics and other functions. A special operations squadron for employment with our Special Forces (SF) is also planned. At present, army aviation has 208 helicopters on its inventory. This is the largest in the similar class of helicopters among the three services.

DHRUV

SA330F PUMA

CH-47 CHINOOK

Army Aviation of Selected Countries

Before discussing what needs to be done to make the AAC a potent force, it may be worthwhile having a brief look at the aviation corps of some of the armies of the world.

Brief details of the aviation corps of the following armies are at following appendices:-

- Appendix 'A' - Army Aviation of USA.
- Appendix 'B' - Army Aviation of UK.
- Appendix 'C' - Army Aviation of France.
- Appendix 'D' - Army Aviation of Pakistan.
- Appendix 'E' - Army Aviation of Australia.
- Appendix 'F' - Army Aviation of other countries.

Future AAC of the Indian Army: Aspects for Consideration

General

We need to be clear about the likely roles AAC would perform in the coming decades, keeping in mind the ongoing changes about how armies will fight wars in future and manage conflicts. It is only then that a coherent picture will emerge regarding the types of structures and organisations we need for the AAC.

The strategic realities of the 21st century are already changing many established norms. Recent events have underscored the uncertainty of the present times. The last decade or so has placed unprecedented operational demands on the army. Proxy war, high-grade insurgency, terrorism and militancy are ongoing challenges. These are in addition to the ever present danger of fighting a conventional war, in the backdrop of a nuclear threat. Civil disturbances, disaster relief, humanitarian and peacekeeping operations, and similar contingencies punctuate the need for a trained and ready contingency-oriented army. Amidst these demands, domestic change and fiscal constraints broaden the challenge.

The immense effect that application of high technology will have in future warfare needs no elaboration. Weapons with the "effects of massed forces" are already available to our potential adversaries. Precision munitions, digital communications, and position location equipment are changing the face of the future battlefield.

Mobility, agility, simultaneity of effort, lethality, increased battle tempo, and space-age logistics will increasingly dominate the army's restructuring initiatives and investment decisions. Intuitive and versatile leaders, supported by agile battle staffs and well-trained soldiers are also essential for future operations.

Characteristics

Army aviation greatly enhances the commander's ability to apply four fundamental principles of war -manoeuvre, mass, surprise, and economy of force. The primary mission of army aviation is to fight the land battle and to support ground operations. Army aviation consists of soldiers; not airmen, and its battlefield leverage is achieved through a combination of reconnaissance, mobility and firepower that is unprecedented in land warfare. Army aviation, as a manoeuvre force, is the third dimension centrepiece of the land force. Reconnaissance, attack, utility and cargo helicopters; complemented by SF, fixed-wing and medical evacuation aircraft; and ATC, are all required to support the army. The range of military operations demands readiness for a wide range of employment.

Expansion of the battlefield is necessary to enable the commander to seize the initiative at a critical point in the battle. Aviation expands the ground commander's battlefield, principally in space and time, by extending the range at which direct fires and observed fires can be concentrated on the enemy, and by expanding his reconnaissance and surveillance envelope, beyond the effective range of other systems. Army aviation expands battle-space at each echelon to which it is assigned, providing a capability where none previously existed or enhancing existing capabilities. Aviation allows commanders to achieve the effects of 'mass' without massing weapons systems.

Army aviation's greatest contribution to battlefield success is the ability it gives the commander to apply decisive combat power at critical times, virtually anywhere on the battlefield. This may be direct fire from aviation manoeuvre units or the insertion of overwhelming infantry forces or artillery fires, delivered into combat via air assault. This versatility is the very essence of army aviation.

Close support missions support ground combat operations. These operations include air movement, command and control; ATC services, EW; close fire support, support by observed fire, combat search and rescue; and aerial mine delivery. The primary function of these missions is to support combat elements in contact with the enemy.

Army aviation performs close service support functions in support of units throughout the entire area of operations. Aviation units enhance the commander's battle-space through rapid delivery of supplies and personnel and aero-medical evacuation.

Army aviation must be prepared for employment throughout the entire range of military operations. Army aviation's contributions to situational awareness are through reconnaissance and security operations, precision engagements, and its ability to rapidly react throughout the spectrum of operations.

Army aviation provides tactical reconnaissance, mobile command, control, communications, and intelligence (C3I); and intelligence warfare/EW to enable the force to gain greater manoeuvre, firepower, and protection for the force.

Helicopter borne (Heliborne) or fixed-wing command posts at brigade, division, corps, and command will give a commander at any level the ability to digitally command and control his assets at extended ranges, as well as the ability to rapidly reposition himself as the situation develops. Battle-space is only limited by a commander's ability to acquire and engage the enemy. Army aviation expands the ground commander's battle-space well beyond the effective range of ground manoeuvre forces at every echelon.

Army aviation provides the commander with real-time intelligence throughout his battle-space with its attack and reconnaissance aircraft. Decisive operations do not require the presence of overwhelming forces, simply the ability to mass overwhelming firepower and other effects at the point where the enemy is most vulnerable. Army aviation gives the commander the ability to see that point and manoeuvre his forces to strike it.

Vision

As we look toward the next 20 to 25 years of this century and the pivotal role army aviation is likely to play across the full range of military operations, it is imperative that we have a vision for the AAC, which will serve to guide its collective thought and actions. A suggested vision is as under:-

"Army Aviation must provide combat, combat support and combat service support capabilities, across the full spectrum of operations, to all field commanders. Its inherent versatility, manoeuvre advantage and effectiveness in battle must influence all dimensions of the future battle-space. Highly motivated aviators, equipped with modern aviation platforms and related systems, and trained to world-class proficiency, must provide commanders at all levels an exponential increase in lethality, a force multiplier of the highest level and a technologically competent leadership, to achieve decisive victory."

Mission

The mission of army aviation must be to find, fix, and destroy the enemy through fire and manoeuvre; and to provide combat support and combat service support in coordinated operations, as an integral member of the combined arms team.

Roles

On the modern battlefield, army aviation, unlike the other members of the combined arms team, has the organic flexibility, versatility, and assets to fulfil a variety of manoeuvre, close support, and close service support roles and functions. These cover the entire spectrum of combined arms operations. Army aviation can accomplish each of these roles–within the limits of its assets and capabilities–during offensive or defensive operations; and also in joint, combined, contingency, or special operations.

The operational roles of army aviation could be listed as under:-

- **Manoeuvre.** During joint and combined arms manoeuvre operations, aviation can execute missions, which include attack against mechanised forces, material and personnel; reconnaissance and surveillance; air assault, aerial security, air combat, special operations, command and control; joint operations and deep operations.
- **Combat Support.** Army aviation should be able to render operational close support assistance in missions, which include C3I, air movement of combat power, aerial mine warfare, search and rescue; ATC services, fire support, and EW.
- **Combat Service Support.** Army aviation should be able to provide assistance to sustain combat forces primarily through air movement of personnel, supplies and equipment; and performing aero-medical evacuation and aviation maintenance. Close service support missions include: intra-theatre airlift; aerial pre-planned and immediate re-

supply; air movement of critically short/ sensitive supplies; pre-positioning and movement of fuel and ammunition; air movement of nuclear and chemical munitions; and relocation of battlefield systems (dismounted infantry, air defence (AD) detachments, engineer stores, equipment, and so on).

Broad Organisational Structures

Army aviation assets are needed at all formations from command level to divisional level. In some cases, there may also be a need to include AAC assets in the order of battle (Orbat) of an independent brigade group. At present, army aviation assets are inadequate for the size of the Indian Army and the tasks it is required to perform. Even the Accretion Plan-2017 appears somewhat modest when the totality of requirements is worked out.

The operational diversities of the Indian Army, coupled with the variety of terrain, extensive deployment in mountainous and high-altitude areas, need for over the crest line observation for reconnaissance by field commanders, direction of artillery fire, cas evac from inaccessible areas and speedy move of commanders to the forward posts which are difficult to access, make the need for a dedicated aviation unit for every infantry and mountain division a necessity.

Mechanised warfare in plains and desert terrain requires the integration of the third dimension with mechanised forces, by way of attack and scout helicopters. All armoured divisions need a dedicated attack helicopter squadron, in addition to an R&O squadron.

It is not the intention of this paper to suggest the future force levels of the AAC, but only to highlight the broad structures that may be needed to make the AAC a potent arm of the Indian Army, so that the combat efficiency of the latter is enhanced to the maximum extent.

The following recommendations are made:-

- AAC must have a mix of both fixed-wing aircraft and helicopters, with the helicopters being in larger numbers.
- Fixed-wing aircraft are needed for communications duties, as airborne command posts, for reconnaissance and surveillance, for cas evac and similar other tasks.
- The helicopter fleet should consist of attack helicopters; armed helicopters (gunship), heavy, medium and light lift utility helicopters; observation helicopters, and helicopters for communications; EW, and as aerial command posts.

- One or more composite squadrons specially dedicated for functioning with the SF.
- Headquarters commands and corps need to have aviation brigades, and divisions should have aviation squadrons. The corps aviation brigade may operate directly under the corps, or be placed under operational control of a subordinate division. The corps commander can task-organise other corps assets, especially division aviation squadrons, under the command of the corps aviation brigade.
- The corps aviation brigade plans, coordinates, and executes aviation operations in support of the corps scheme of manoeuvre. It can be expected to operate anywhere in the corps area.
- The corps aviation brigade should conduct attack and reconnaissance operations to find, fix, and destroy enemy forces. It should also conduct security, air assault, command and control, and air movement operations throughout the corps area of operations.
- The division aviation squadron should conduct all aviation combat, close support and close service support missions (except fixed-wing operations) in support of the division scheme of manoeuvre. The primary mission of the division aviation squadron should be to find, fix, and destroy enemy forces within the division area. The division aviation squadron will usually accomplish such missions as a part of a task-organised force.

Conclusion

Army aviation's strength is in its ability to deploy quickly, conduct reconnaissance and surveillance; manoeuvre rapidly, and focus tremendous combat power for the land forces' commander. Army aviation gives the land forces' commanders unique capabilities that enhance their force's overall effectiveness.

Army aviation's mobility and firepower make it a dominant force, a force that can gain and maintain contact, and destroy the enemy in depth, allowing him no safe haven in which to reorganise, rearm, or recover. Attack and reconnaissance helicopter units give the commander a force that can rapidly build devastating firepower at any point on the battlefield.

Army aviation must have a high degree of battle-space mobility, so as to greatly increase the probability that aviation units will be at the right place, at the right time, and with the right capabilities required, to meet the commander's objectives. Army aviation's strength must be its versatility to deploy quickly, see the battlefield, manoeuvre rapidly, and focus tremendous combat power (such as artillery and air force assets) at decisive points.

Army aviation needs to develop organisations that enhance aviation capabilities to support the concepts of operations of field commanders. The force structure should be tailored to meet evolving tactical requirements. In addition, aviation organisations should include appropriate maintenance and logistical support elements required to sustain the force.

On-board communications on AAC platforms need to possess a low probability of intercept, provide a jam-resistant capability, and hardening against virtually any source of electronic countermeasures (ECM), and operate in both secure and non-secure modes.

Army aviation command and control headquarters (brigade and squadron) will need to have the capability to communicate (voice, data, and imagery) with AD, air traffic services, field artillery, air force, and navy. Army aviation command and control headquarters should also have the capability to communicate with other friendly forces over all types of terrain and through virtually any level of battlefield clutter and aural or electronic interference.

Aviation leadership development should be expanded to prepare aviation leaders for the diverse challenges that this versatile force requires.

Finally, the changing features of technology should be brought into focus for the soldier to acquire and master the skills necessary to win and survive on the battlefield of the future. Each facet of doctrine, training, leader development, organisation, and logistics needs to interface with the individual and collective abilities of the soldiers to which these capabilities will be applied. Technology will capitalise on the inherent capabilities of soldiers, who will use it optimally. The format and content of the technology presented to the soldier must be intuitive and standardised to enhance decision-making skills. ■

Appendix 'A'

US Army Aviation

Introduction

US Army Aviation had its beginning in 1909, when the signal corps raised its first aeronautical division. In 1912, the US Artillery commenced using aircraft for spotter tasks. World War II witnessed two aspects of army aviation role, the air corps or air force role, and the light aviation role. As with the case of USA, air forces of many countries are an offshoot of their army aviation.

US Army Aviation first tasted combat on November 9, 1942 in the North African campaign of World War II, where small, light, fixed-wing L-4s acted as artillery spotters, aerial cargo re-suppliers, air ambulances and command and control aircraft.

The birth of rotary-wing flight is credited to Igor Sikorsky, who in 1941 flew the first contraption that remotely resembled that which we know today as the helicopter.

The first test of the application of the helicopter in combat came during the Korean War. The star attraction was the H-13 Sioux. Although the army employed both fixed and rotary-wing aircraft in Korea, the helicopter was best suited to give direct support to the soldiers in the field, who were isolated due to the mountainous terrain and lack of fixed facilities and runways.

The Vietnamese Experience

The jungles of Vietnam and the advent of guerrilla warfare proved to be the true test of US Army Aviation and the concept of organic tactical mobility. In Vietnam, the helicopter was universally employed for various missions, including attack, air assault, aerial re-supply, medical evacuation, aerial reconnaissance, and command and control. The venerable UH-1H was the backbone of most operations in Southeast Asia. It was the Huey, converted into a gunship that was the first helicopter to deliver ordnance in combat and gave birth to the attack helicopter concept. The 1st Cavalry Division (Airmobile) was deployed in Vietnam in July 1965.

In 1967, it was the 2nd Airmobile Division, 101st Airborne, which was deployed in Vietnam, where it merged with its predecessor sister unit, the 1st Aviation Brigade, to eventually form one of the largest (approximately 4,000 aircraft) brigade commands in Vietnam. In 1967, the AH-1 Cobra gunship was also introduced. The Cobra was a highly manoeuvrable and very lethal weapons platform. It was the first of its kind, a helicopter designed specifically for the ground attack mission by aviation units. By 1968-69, the Cobra was fully integrated into army aviation units, fighting alongside and above the infantry, giving new meaning to "close air support".

Army aviation performed extremely well in three major operations in Vietnam. These were the Tet offensive of January-February 1968; the relief of Khe Sahn by the 1st Cavalry in 1968; and LAMSON 719 in February 1971, which supported South Vietnamese troops in Laos. All these operations were unique in that they all employed helicopter gunships. Army aviation also played a sterling role in medical evacuation in Vietnam, where it was instrumental in saving over 320,000 US soldiers' lives by helicopter medical evacuation.

Modernisation and Transformation

The 1973 Yom Kippur War, with awesome high-tech lethal weapons, reshaped US Army Aviation thinking. Surface-to-air missiles (SAM's), with sophisticated acquisition systems; and the need to operate without air superiority, changed the concept of future operations. Army aviators commenced flying low nap-of-the-earth (NOE) flight modes, to avoid target acquisition and lethal SAM engagements.

Technological advances in composites structures, night-vision optics and infrared (IR) target acquisition and detection systems have now enabled army aviation to develop and field more survivable and lethal aircraft. US Army Aviation now owns the night-deploying, employing and fighting a majority of all missions at night, at treetop altitudes and in adverse weather.

US Army Aviation has approximately 4,813 helicopters, consisting of 1,294 attack/ armed, 2,045 light/ medium utility and 1,075 other helicopters. It has 18 aviation brigades. There are 269 helicopters in the air assault division, 131 in heavy division and 97 in a light division.

Aviation Organisations

The aviation brigade is common to all heavy and light active divisions of the US Army. It is considered a manoeuvre brigade and is normally designated the fourth brigade in most divisions. It is designed to fight, command, and allocate aviation forces. The typical brigade consists of 131 aircraft, with a headquarters and headquarters company (HHC), a cavalry squadron (with air and ground assets), a command aviation company (CAC), an assault helicopter company (AHC) and one or two attack helicopter battalions. Forward deployed brigades have two attack helicopter battalions. Details of units are as under:-

- The HHC has a full staff complement for executing all staff functions, including issue of plans and orders.
- The cavalry squadron serves as the eyes and ears of the division. Its missions include reconnaissance, deployment of screens, and command and control enhancement. The squadron consists of a headquarters and headquarters troop, two ground cavalry troops, and two air reconnaissance troops. It has a total of 55 ground vehicles (15 X M113s and 40 Bradleys) and 21 aircraft. Each air troop has four AH-1s and six OH-58s, with one UH-60 in the headquarters.
- The AHC is the primary organic air mover of the division. It has 18 X UH-60s, grouped in three flight platoons.
- The CAC provides special electronic mission aircraft and field artillery observers for the division.
- The attack helicopter battalion is employed only as a battalion size force and companies are not separately employed. Its mission is to destroy armour and mechanised targets with mobility, firepower and shock effect.

An attack helicopter battalion consists of three attack companies with six AH-64 each.

In the light divisions, brigade organisational structure includes an HHC, a reconnaissance squadron, two AHCs and one attack helicopter battalion.

The aviation brigade of the air assault division is significantly bigger, with four attack helicopter battalions, a medium lift aviation battalion (CH-47), a command aviation battalion, an air reconnaissance squadron, a medical evacuation battalion and an aviation maintenance battalion. Total aircraft number 327. The 101st Airborne-Air Assault Division is the only formation with this organisation.

The organic aviation unit in an armoured cavalry regiment is the Regimental Aviation Squadron (RAS). It has two attack helicopter troops, three air reconnaissance troops, and an assault helicopter troop. A total of 72 aircraft are assigned to it.

Additional corps level aviation organisational structures are activated during war, with operational assets that include the corps aviation brigade, with two attack helicopter regiments and an aviation group. The corps aviation brigade may operate directly for the corps commander or be placed under operational control of a subordinate division. The corps commander can allocate other corps assets, especially division aviation units, under the command of the corps aviation brigade or task the corps aviation brigade to support an armoured cavalry regiment.

The aviation brigade may also be tasked to be a covering force headquarters, when augmented by ground forces. The corps aviation brigade conducts attack and reconnaissance operations to find, fix, and destroy enemy forces; it also conducts security, air assault, command and control, and air movement operations throughout the corps area of operations. The corps aviation brigade plans, coordinates, and executes aviation operations in support of the corps scheme of manoeuvre. It can be expected to operate anywhere in the corps area.

The division aviation brigade conducts all aviation combat, close support and close service support missions (except ATS and fixed-wing operations) in support of the division scheme of manoeuvre. The primary mission of the division aviation brigade is to find, fix, and destroy enemy forces within the division area. The division aviation brigade can accomplish this mission as an aviation-pure or task-organised force. The combination of infantry, armour and aviation, at the division level, are required for operations, in depth, throughout the course of battle, to fight combined arms battles. Therefore, combat aviation must be primarily assigned to, and employed by, divisional aviation brigades, just as infantry and armour battalions are assigned to, and employed by, their parent brigades.

Rotary-Wing Aircraft

Major rotary-wing aircraft in the US Army Aviation corps are as under:-

- **AH-64 Apache Advanced Attack Helicopter.** This twin-engine fighter is a unique weapons system. A pilot night-vision system enables the crew to fly and fight the Apache at night without artificial illumination. An advanced target acquisition designation system (TADS) enables the crew to detect and engage simultaneous targets at standoff weapons ranges. It is armed with the 16 laser-designated Hellfire missile, capable of engaging numerous armour targets from concealed positions, to ranges up to seven km. The Apache is also armed with a 30mm chain gun (1,500m) and 2.75 inch folding-fin (or free-flight) aircraft rocket (FFAR) system (10 km). The Apache is as survivable as it is lethal. A ballistic blast shield separates the two-crew compartments. Its transmission can operate without oil for 30 minutes before failure.
- **AH-1 Cobra.** First fielded in the late 1960s at the end of the Vietnam War,

the Cobra is armed with up to eight wire-guided Tow missiles (3,750m), 38 X 2.75 inch FFARs and 20mm Gatling gun (1,000m, 750 rounds). The Cobra is a very capable and deadly tank killer. The AH-1 has a crew of two -a pilot and co-pilot/ gunner.

- **CH-47 Chinook Heavy Lift Helicopter.** The Chinook has dual rotors. It can lift 28,000 pounds or 33 combat loaded troops. The Chinook is the heavy-lift workhorse of the aviation fleet. The Chinook is capable of transporting an entire Forward Arming and Replenishment Point (FAARP) for deep operations, or lift two 155mm cannons with ammunition and crew.
- **OH-58 Kiowa Aerial Scout.** It is a general-purpose light observation helicopter, which is adaptable for various light duty missions, like command and control, reconnaissance, light re-supply, forward observation and security. It is manned by a single pilot, but carries a co-pilot/ navigator, commander, forward observer or aerial observer, as dictated by the mission. In cavalry and attack battalions, the OH-58 is normally armed with a pair of Stinger air-to-air missiles (AAM's). It is assigned to almost all units as a general-purpose/ light observation aircraft.
- **The OH-58D Kiowa Warrior.** It functions as the advanced aerial scout with high-powered day TV and IR optics, laser-designator/ tracker and an inertial navigation system. The mast mounted sight feature of the OH-58D allows the aircraft to remain concealed during observation and target designation. The Warrior's cockpit is a combination of state-of-the-art electronic displays and digital communication packages. Equipped with the latest communications equipment, the Warrior is capable of non-verbal, data burst transmissions with Apaches and field artillery units. The OH-58D can be configured with the Stinger, Hellfire (2), 2.75 inch FFARs (14), or .50 cal machine guns.
- **UH-1 Iroquois or "Hue".** It is a general-purpose medium lift aircraft suitable for aerial re-supply, air assaults (eight troops) and command and control, with a payload of 2,900 pounds. It has a crew of three -pilot, co-pilot and flight engineer. This helicopter is the backbone of the army aviation fleet.
- **UH-60 Black Hawk**. It is a multi-purpose medium lift helicopter. The Black Hawk is a twin-engine, fully instrumented workhorse; capable of carrying 13 fully-loaded combat troops. It normally has a crew of three - pilot, co-pilot and flight engineer. With an external payload of 8,000

pounds, the Black Hawk hauls a wide array of battlefield systems, to include howitzers and light vehicles. For combat, the Black Hawk is armed with twin door-mounted M-60 machine guns.

Fixed-Wing Aircraft

The US Army also operates approximately 450 fixed-wing aircraft, which are employed in a variety of support roles. ■

Appendix 'B'

Army Aviation of UK

Introduction

Following significant developments during World War II, the AAC formally joined the army orbat in the early 1950s. Since then its place on the battlefield has developed rapidly as an integral element of the army's manoeuvre forces. The introduction of attack helicopters clearly indicated the shift of emphasis from combat support towards the combat role, particularly within air manoeuvre operations. However, despite this changing emphasis, the army also has a continuing essential requirement for army aviation to provide both combat support and combat service support roles.

Army aviation operations rely for their effect on integration into combined arms groupings (e.g. brigades and battle groups), of which army aviation forms an element, the most pivotal of which is its place within air manoeuvre forces. In the context of land operations, air manoeuvre seeks decisive advantage through the exploitation of the third dimension by combined arms forces centred on rotary-wing aircraft, but within an overall joint operations framework.

Organisation

The AAC of UK is placed directly under the general staff and is controlled through the Headquarters Directorate of Army Aviation, which is akin to the Additional Directorate General Army Aviation of the Indian Army. All aspects of the AAC, including its organisation, concepts and doctrine; operations, training of air/ ground crew; air worthiness, standardisation, trials, equipment, maintenance, logistics and recruiting are controlled by this headquarters. In addition, it deals with regimental matters and the army aviation museum.

The combined operations environment of ground and air elements created by the formation of 16 Air Assault Brigade recently has created a need to merge the command and control elements of AAC regiments and Royal Air Force (RAF) troop and vehicle carrying support helicopters in the forward combat zone. The integration of aviation attack and combat support assets has been made possible by the formation of the Joint Helicopter Command (JHC), whose role is to deliver and sustain effective battlefield helicopters and air assault assets, operationally capable under all environmental conditions, to support all UK defence missions and tasks. In addition to AAC aviation assets, JHC also commands all RAF support helicopters and all naval helicopters used by the Royal Marines.

Although the AAC operates some fixed-wing aircraft for training, liaison flying and radar duties, the main effort goes into providing helicopter support for the ground forces. About 350 AAC helicopters are used for anti-tank operations, artillery fire control, reconnaissance, liaison flying and a limited troop lift. The current attack helicopter in service with the AAC is the Lynx, with Tow missiles, but a new attack helicopter is due to be inducted shortly.

The AAC has approximately 3,200 personnel, including approximately 544 trained pilots.

Mission

- **Combat Aviation.** To find, fix and strike, either independently, or as the lead element, or as a constituent of combined arms groupings, throughout the depth of the battlefield and the 24-hour battle, and throughout the full spectrum of operations.
- **Combat Support Aviation.** To provide enabling capabilities for combined arms operations, throughout the depth of the battlefield and the 24-hour battle, and throughout the full spectrum of operations.

Roles

- **In Combat.** To conduct air manoeuvre using direct fire and manoeuvre, as part of the land battle component.
- **In Combat Support.** To provide ISTAR (Integrated, Surveillance, Target Acquisition Radar), as a collection asset in its own right or potentially as a platform for other sensors, including ECM; NBC reconnaissance; ESM (electronic support measures); radar and other electronic systems.

Other Tasks

- To provide direction of fire support (ground/ air/ maritime/ SF).
- To provide mobility for combat forces.
- To assist in command and control, including acting as airborne command posts.
- To provide a limited extrication capability.

- To provide movement for personnel and material including cas evac in a combat service support role.

Tasks of Army Aviation

- **Attack Aviation.** Aviation attack regiments are equipped with both attack and utility helicopters. Their primary role is to provide the firepower and enabling capabilities around which combined arms manoeuvre operations can be conducted. Attack helicopters are a manoeuvre weapon system, and have three main tasks as under: -
  - ◻ Attack tasks.
  - ◻ Armed reconnaissance tasks.
  - ◻ Security tasks.

- **Combat Support Aviation.** These tasks are undertaken by light utility helicopters in two inter-related categories as under: -

◻ **In support of Attack Helicopters.** Light utility helicopters provide the primary means to undertake battle procedures in support of the attack helicopter element. In so doing, they equate to the ground vehicles that support battle procedures within armoured regiments. Examples of light utility helicopter tasks in direct support of attack aviation are:-

- As an integral element of aviation missions.
- For forward operating base/ FAARP as a precursor to a full ground reconnaissance.
- Movement between forward operating base/ FAARP etc. of aircrew, attack helicopter role equipment, ordnance and so on.

◻ In Support of other Elements of the Field Army. Where limited forces are required to control large areas, domination by observation and a physical presence in the air can be the most efficient and effective way of conducting manoeuvres. Typically these tasks include:-

- Deployment and recovery of discrete tactical groups, particularly in the preparatory stages of manoeuvre operations such as engineer reconnaissance and preparation parties; special patrols insertion/ extrication; harbour parties; AD detachments etc.
- *Command.* The movement of a commander to the right place in battle whilst retaining command during high tempo operations. Divisional, brigade and battle group commanders can be supported in this way.

- *Communications.* Light utility helicopters can be employed as a communications platform providing radio relay and re-broadcast.
- *Command and Control Support.* Light utility helicopters provide a means of rapid movement between headquarters and units for key command and control staff and equipment. They also provide a relatively secure method for transporting classified and security material (e.g. crypto).
- *Control of Fire.* Although the control of fire can be carried out from attack helicopters, light utility helicopters can also be used to provide this capability, in support of both ground and air manoeuvre forces.
- Light utility helicopters provide mobility for forward observation officer (FOO) parties, artillery tactical groups and forward air controller (FAC) parties, within the forward battle area. Light utility helicopter crews also undertake fire control duties when FOO and FAC parties are unavailable. This is also applicable to attack helicopter crews, but it is unlikely that attack helicopters will be available for these tasks in support of ground manoeuvre.
- Light utility helicopters also provide airborne fire control for Joint Air Attack Team (JAAT) operations.
- *ISTAR Support.* Light utility helicopters provide a form of manned reconnaissance, whereby the crew, together with their observation devices are capable of acquiring information, interpreting it, and reacting to that information. Some examples of light utility helicopter ISTAR tasks are: screens, observation posts, point reconnaissance, route reconnaissance; area reconnaissance, battlefield damage assessment. Examples of ISTAR support tasks are: formation and battle group reconnaissance, engineer reconnaissance, AD reconnaissance, NBC reconnaissance.
- *Combat Recovery.* Light utility helicopters can be used for the recovery, not just of aircrew, but of all military personnel. This may be undertaken through a formal process, but may also be an immediate ad-hoc task undertaken on behalf of a supported unit or formation.
- *Sustainment.* A wide range of tasks can be undertaken by light utility helicopters in sustaining formations and units. Some require tactical movement in forward areas where the relatively small size of light utility helicopters is an advantage. Others, although relatively straightforward transport tasks, are more suited to light utility helicopters when movement by larger transport helicopter would be unwieldy or impractical. Examples of sustainment tasks for light utility helicopters are: cas evac, movement of individuals or small parties; movement of freight such as ordnance or ammunition within the forward battle area. ■

Appendix 'C'

Army Aviation of France

Introduction

Army aviation of France was established on November 22, 1954, with the roles of observation, reconnaissance, assault and supply duties. A three star General heads the French Army Aviation now.

Orqanisation

The major combat element of the French Army Aviation is an air mobile brigade. It has four combat helicopter regiments, each of which comprises:-

- One headquarter squadron.
- One supply and provision squadron.
- One reconnaissance squadron.
- One or two strike helicopter squadrons.
- Three attack helicopter squadrons.
- One assault transport and heavy lift squadron.

Regional liaison squadrons are designated *Groupe d'Helicopteres Lagers* (GHL).

Specialised army aviation comprises SF units and army aviation units operating in foreign countries. They are capable of performing heliborne operations by sea and intelligence gathering tasks.

The French Army School of Aviation is the nodal agency to conduct training for all helicopter pilots in the French Defence Forces and also caters for the training requirements of air Force, navy and the Gendarmerie.

The following aspects of the French Army Aviation are of interest:-

- It is a combat arm; with SF units capable of performing operations by sea.
- All helicopter pilots in France are directly trained on helicopters only.
- Extensive use of simulators greatly assists in operational training of aircrew.

Aircraft Inventory

Total aviation assets, predominantly helicopters and a few fixed-wing aircraft consist of 424 aircraft, of which approximately 202 are attack/ armed helicopters. The inventory consists of Eurocopter Tiger HAC/ HAP, SA 342 L1/ M

Gazelle, AS 532 M Super Puma, AS 532 UL Cougar Horizon, SA 341 C/ F/ H Gazelle, SOCATA TBM-700, SA 330 B/ H Puma SOCAT, NHI NH 90 TTH, Cessna F406 Caravan II, AS 555 UN Fennec and Pilatus PC-6B Turbo Porter.

Eurocopter Tiger attack helicopter had entered service in 2003, with eventual requirement for 214 helicopters. ■

Army Aviation of Pakistan

Introduction

Pakistan Army, though half the size of the Indian Army, has more than double the army aviation assets. Pakistan has 21 army aviation squadrons, while the Indian Army has only 11 army aviation squadrons. Pakistan Army Aviation has over 400 aircraft.

Pakistan Army Aviation had five squadrons in 1971. These grew to 18 by 1987, 19 by 1991 and 21 now.

Organisation

Army Aviation of Pakistan consists of the following types of units:-

- **Combat Squadrons.** The two combat squadrons are equipped with AH-1S (Huey Cobra) attack helicopters, scout and utility helicopters.
- **Composite Aviation Squadrons.** There are 12 composite army aviation squadrons, each with three fixed-wing flights and one rotary-wing flight.
- **Utility Squadrons.** There are four utility squadrons, each with two logistics flights of Mi-8/ Puma and Allouette III helicopters.
- Cargo Squadrons. Pakistan has raised three cargo squadrons equipped with Mi-8/ Puma helicopters and light observation helicopters.

Aviation Assets

The types of aircraft and numbers in the inventory are as under:-

• **Fixed-Wing Aircraft.** MFI-17/ L-19/ O-1/ SAAB/ YAK-3 (Transport Aircraft).	-	224
• **Attack Helicopters.** AH 1S (Huey Cobra).	-	19
• **Cargo (Medium Lift).** Mi-17/ Mi-8/ Puma.	-	54
• Light Observation/ Utility Helicopters. Bell 205/ 206/ 212/ Allouette III/ 315 B Lama	-	116
Total	-	**413**

Army Aviation of Australia

In 1986, the Chiefs of Staff Committee decided that all battlefield helicopters, with no size or weight limitations, would be transferred to the army. The following year, 5 Aviation Regiment was raised and the Sikorsky S-70A Black Hawk helicopter entered service. In January 1989, the command of 5 Aviation Regiment was transferred to the army and its A and B Squadrons were raised, with Black Hawk helicopters for troop lift and Bell UH-1H Iroquois helicopters as gunship. In 1990, the Australian Defence Force (ADF) Helicopter School was raised. In 1998, the Army Aviation Training Centre was formed to command the School of Army Aviation, the Helicopter School and the Aircraft Maintenance School. In 2000, commander divisional aviation, a colonel-level appointment was created to command the two aviation regiments, and in 2001, aviation capability development group was created to introduce new capabilities. The first of their projects is the armed reconnaissance helicopter.

The Australian AAC is now manned by 337 officers and 232 other rank. It comprises the Army Aviation Training Centre with two schools - the Army Helicopter School and the School of Army Aviation, and 16 Aviation Brigade with two regiments; 1 and 5 Aviation Regiments. The corps has a total inventory of 114 aircraft, which includes six Chinooks, 36 Black Hawks, 25 Iroquois, and 42 Kiowa Warrior with three King Air Twin Otters on lease. The Australian Army Aviation has a potent army aviation manoeuvre capability. Over the next decade, it will absorb the armed reconnaissance helicopter (the Eurocopter Tiger), an additional troop lift squadron, and will be involved in the introduction of tactical unmanned aerial vehicles (UAVs). ■

Army Aviation of Other Countries

China

The People's Liberation Army (PLA) exercises overall command and control over all armed forces. China does not have army aviation as a separate air arm, since the PLA Air Force (PLAAF) functions directly under the Chief of General Staff of the General Staff Department of the PLA.

China has six army aviation regiments, holding approximately 321 aircraft in its inventory. These comprise 124 attack/ armed helicopters, 181 light/ medium utility helicopters and 36 others.

Russia

Russia has approximately 20 helicopter regiments. Each command and corps level formations have a helicopter regiment each, consisting of 110 and 80 helicopters respectively. Divisional level formations have helicopter support squadrons.

The Russian inventory of helicopters is approximately 1,700. These consist of 708 attack/ armed helicopters, approximately 1,500 light/ medium/ utility helicopters and 140 other types.

Germany

Each German corps has an army aviation command and each division has an army aviation squadron.

The inventory of helicopters in the German Army is approximately 568. These consist of 302 attack/ armed helicopters, approximately 322 light/ medium utility helicopters and 42 other types. ■

Historic Overview of Army Aviation

— **Rear Admiral K. Raja Menon**

In all armed forces of the world, the act of flying into the air first translated itself militarily into occupying a height for observation of the enemy. This activity was, in every country undertaken by a branch of the army. In the World War I, some very primitive bombing occurred from the air, to prevent which defensive fighters engaged in dog fights with the bombing aircraft. By the end of the World War I, the Royal Flying Corps (RFC) of Great Britain was the largest air force in the world with approximately 3,500 aircraft of all kinds.

The oldest air force in the world is the German Luftwaffe, which was disbanded in 1918 as a result of the armistice. The RAF, from which we trace our own flying heritage, was formed as the RFC in 1912 to replace the air battalion operated by the Royal Engineers. The RFC was still an army organisation, but was transferred into the RAF in April 1918. This force also included the naval air branch which was returned to the Royal Navy in 1937.

During the war, the Royal Indian Air Force was also formed and first saw action in Mesopotamia under the operational command of the Indian Army in Iraq for almost seven years until 1922.The reason for going into the history of the RAF is that, most of the combat flying in the world owe their origin to one of three parent flying service is namely:-

- **The RAF.** It is the parent organisation of all commonwealth air forces.
- **The US Army Air Force.** The USAAF formed the parent organisation for many of the western non-commonwealth air forces, except France, and also for the Japanese and Taiwanese army and air forces.
- **The Soviet Air Force.** The Soviets influenced the combat flying arrangements of all former communist countries, including China.

If one looks at the different ways in which each country organised its air, missiles and combat flying arrangements, one comes across a bewildering amount of differences. But since we have to concentrate on army aviation, it is necessary to look at the manner in which different countries looked at army aviation, as separate or integral to the air force.

The biggest different between what may be called the British or the RAF heritage and the US heritage is that in the UK, the RAF was the holding service for all flying activities, while in the USA , it was the army which had the air force as it's part until 1947 or so. During the World War II, the US air power was deployed as the USAAF. The intellectual and doctrinal changes that forced the US Government to concede a separate air force at the end of the World War II are contained in many books. But the important factor to understand is that the intellectual underpinnings to the creation of a separate air force in the USA were based on the strategic bombing campaigns on Germany and Japan. Even today, the US strategic bombing studies are the best military histories that one can refer to on the conduct of a strategic air campaign. The reason for my stressing this factor was that the USAF was always conceived as a strategic force with its fundamental rationale affecting the conduct of total war by the US as a country. Hence the USAF right from the beginning concerned itself primarily with strategic bombing, strategic reconnaissance, strategic airlift, space activities, airborne and space based EW, surveillance and C3I. What I am emphasising here is that when the USAF was spun off from the US Army, the last thing on the minds of the senior USAF intellectuals was any concern with owning the tactical battle-winning air assets, and least of all, battle influencing helicopters. The reason for my stressing this is that all air forces that took their strategic rationale from the USAF seem never to have had a problem with the army's ownership of helicopters, whereas all commonwealth air forces have traditionally had this problem, except of course for Pakistan's, where the army does what it wants to anyway.

The sponsors of this conference have provided a good Approach paper, which describes the experiences of the various air forces with regard to the AAC. I will expand on three and try to give you an overview before narrating what seems to be happening in India.

The US Example

The first example of an integral air cavalry unit comes in 1965 when it was decided politically to intervene in South Vietnam. The old 1st Cavalry Division fought in World War II as a virtual infantry formation. In 1965, the 1st Division was designated as the 1st Airmobile Division and sent to Vietnam. The only air part of this division was the 1st Squadron of 9th Cavalry, which did only reconnaissance and command and control tasks. Its success at the Battle of la Drang was followed by divisional air cavalry companies being formed in four divisions - the 1st, 4th, 9th and 25th Infantry Divisions. Their successes led to the formation of the 1st Aviation Brigade whose organisation is given below.

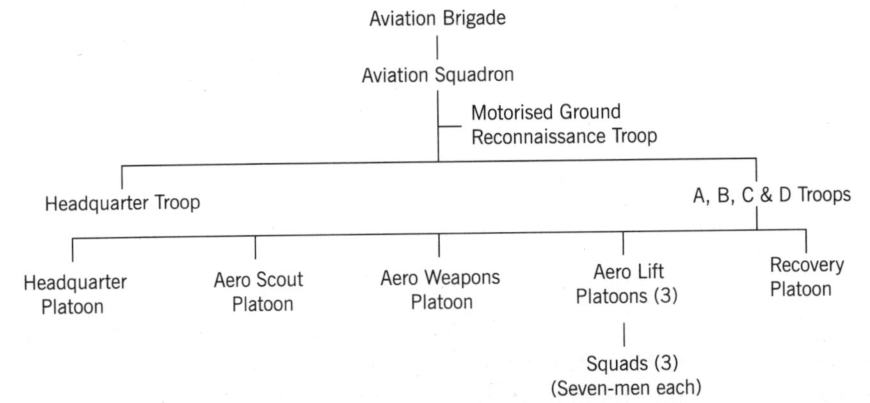

Fig. 1: Organisation of US 1st Aviation Brigade (1966).

The reason for showing you this organisation chart is that in 1966, 40 years ago, this is how airmobile operations started - namely the use of the infantry inserted into battle quickly in advanced positions, supported by helicopter fire. This may have been successful in the jungles of Vietnam, and indeed may be successful in the context of our northeast, but this is not how air cavalry units are organised for warfare in the plains. To understand what army aviation is essentially about, it would be necessary to look at the organisation of the 1st Air Cavalry Division meant to create an armoured break through which is as under:-

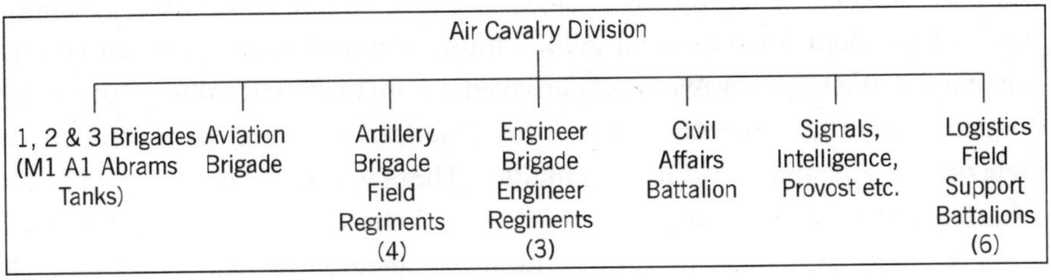

Fig. 2: Organisation of US Air Cavalry Division.

What you would be probably interested in is what the composition is of the aviation brigade which is given below:-

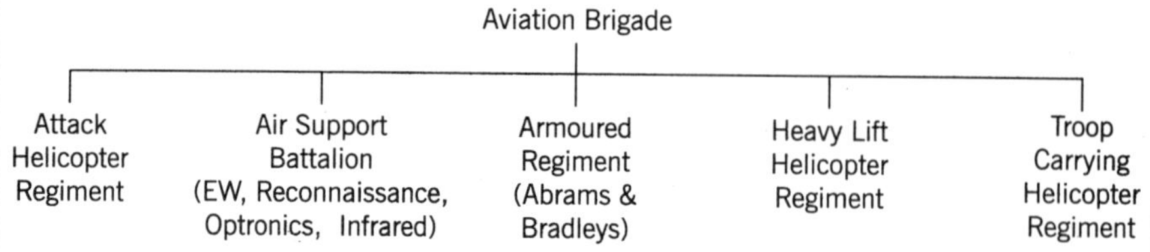

Fig. 3: Organisation of an US Aviation Brigade.

The reason for delving you the mainstay of US Army Aviation is to indicate that the ground and air units are integrated in one command, co-located, which train and fight together. Now quite obviously, if the ground organisation is like this, there is no question that one service has to own both air and ground units, they must be in the same uniform and train and fight together. My reason for stressing this is that if there is a belief that an aviation asset can be with corps headquarters and can be 'allocated' to any infantry division or cavalry formation during combat. If that is the prevailing army philosophy, I think it is a poor philosophy. In any case, it will be a loosing argument because this kind of support can be provided by the air force, and it becomes difficult for the army to justify the case. Because if an asset is allocated by the corps commander and is located in some back area, why can't it be manned and flown by the air force. This may not satisfy the army but it is a reality.

The Australian Experience

There is a good reason for taking up the Australian example. Although the Australian Army is small, because the Australians started their experience with army aviation exactly like us and the British–Air OPs and nothing else initially. The Australians however went into Vietnam with the Americans and the Vietnam experience completely changed the way they looked at army aviation. The independent Australian battalions found themselves in many situations when it was the US Army Aviation that saved it from heavy casualties. During the Vietnam operations the Australian Army Aviation expanded to acquire strike helicopters, EW and troop lift capabilities. There was however a mix of army aviation and Royal Australian Air Force (RAAF) helicopters supporting the army until in 1986 the chiefs of staff committee sat and decided to transfer all 'battlefield helicopters' to the army aviation. So at one go the army got 46 Black Hawks and 26 Iroquois helicopters.

The army raised the first aviation regiment in 1989 at an air force base. In 1990, the Australian Defence Helicopter School was also set up at an old RAAF base, but army pilots did their basic flying with civilian contractors. Today, the Australian Army has an aviation brigade under which are two flying training schools and two aviation regiments. The brigade is about to expand to take the Eurocopter reconnaissance squadron and the UAV squadron.

The UK Experience

I am not sure whether the UK experience is a good one for us to emulate because they went through a completely different reorganisation before they reached into their present organisation, but nevertheless, I will discuss that.

In the UK, all common use helicopters have been formed together into one JHC under a rotating two-star command from each of the services. This command was established in 1999 and obviously is useful to all the three services. The organisation tree of the joint command is given below:-

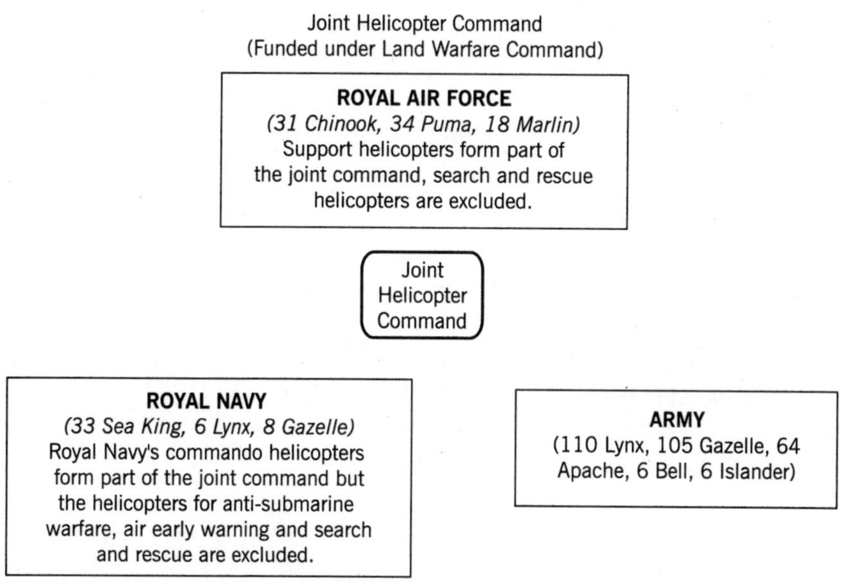

Fig. 4: Joint Helicopter Command of UK.

The Indian Experience

Most of the audience wouldn't need to know any of the basic facts regarding the Indian experience, so I will start with the date that everyone believes is the start point for the Indian experience, namely 1986, the date of the agreement between the air force, the army and presumably the MoD on setting up army aviation. That agreement gave the combat helicopters, funded by the army to be flown by the air force but placed under the operational control of the army, in war. The army would have its own utility helicopters, manned and controlled by it. This is an important agreement and I was not privy to its contents earlier, when I spoke at the Special Forces' seminar conducted by CLAWS. I was then under the impression that the inability of the army to insert SF at night into enemy terrain, at low-level, lay basically with the air force. But I now see that since 1986, nothing really stopped the army from having its own night-flying, commando carrying helicopters. Today, the army aviation has grown to 180 Chetaks and Cheetahs and two squadrons of ALHs. This component makes it the seventh largest AAC after the USA, Russia, China, Germany, France and UK.

It is interesting that the reason given in the Approach Paper for the obstacles in the way of the growth of army aviation lists them as:

- Opposition from the air force.
- Insufficient interest from the army hierarchy.
- Lack of vision in the army.
- Financial constraints.

I have looked at these reasons and spoken to a number of officers from the air force and the army and what emerges are the following amplifications.

Oppositions from the Air Force

It is an old tactic of the non-specialist bureaucrats of the MoD in India that when one service wants something funded, and that affects the other service even in a roundabout way, the file is sent to the other service, which often comments adversely on the sister service's proposal. Under this clause the air force has certainly objected to the following being acquired by the army.

- Fixed-wing aircraft.
- Attack helicopters not manned by the IAF.
- EW and surveillance aircraft of any kind.
- Heavy lift helicopters.

The objections have been on the grounds that these functions are performed by the air force and the army getting into these functions would cause duplication, confusion and make it impossible to perform airspace management.

It is important to look at some more of the criticisms levelled by senior air force officers and some of these include the following.

Quite often the army has a requirement for some kind of air support or rather, the execution of which can only be done from the air. Very often the army then calls the air force for a particular kind of aircraft, and the air force objects, saying that the specialisation of mission planning and the use of specialised aircraft in the business of the air force, and it should not worry the army whether the target is destroyed by helicopter or fixed wing aircraft. An example often quoted is the army's request for attack helicopters in Kargil, when the air force contends that only laser-guided bombs from fixed wing aircraft could have and eventually did the job. The air force contention is that if the army had a choice it would have limited its own air effort to machine gunning from the air.

The other air force criticism is that only the air force has a planned career path that teaches pilots the strategy and tactics of air power as they rise in the service and that flying light helicopters for any number of years does not prepare an army officer to understand the intricacies of the use of air power in complex situations. This objection has been repeatedly raised by respected senior air force officers who say that flying attack helicopters is basically a fighter pilot function. If the air force continued to man attack helicopters, the career paths of these pilots would be protected. In the US Army the attack helicopter pilot corps is big enough to provide an independent career path. This is not so in India where the number of attack helicopters would be small and active service in these helicopters would not lead to a career enhancing posting in the army. I am aware that the army contests this accusation and feels that an attack helicopter officer would be accommodated in the general staff career path like any land warfare specialist.

There is also an apprehenion in the air force that the army expanding into combat helicopter flying is only a foot in the door and could eventually lead to the raising of an independent air force.

To these criticisms, the army has replied to the effect that the army does not wish to expand army aviation in an open ended way but there is a need, at the moment to have what the army calls 'battlefield helicopters' under its own command for training, basing and fighting.

As an outsider to this situation what strikes me are two things. One, about the IAF's desire to retain battlefield helicopters is how an air force can ever get into the strategic air and space business if it is going to get bogged down seriously in the tactical land battle. To explain this further, let me say that every significant air force derives most of its significant doctrine from what the IAF would call 'bomber pilots'. Ever since the Canberras were retired and not replaced, the one question the IAF has to ask is whether the doctrine of the air force has not shifted significantly and perhaps wrongly into getting too involved in the tactical land battle at the cost of its strategic role. If this is the case, then the question to ask is whether a basic shift in the air force's role into a strategic one wouldn't automatically mean getting out of the business of battlefield helicopters, and hence having to object to Army Aviation Accretion Plan-2017.

The other thing that strikes me about the army aviation's case for expansion is that nowhere was I able to find a strong strategic rationale, that would obviously benefit the country – rather than the AAC or the army. During the last 10 years, it was obvious to any writer on strategic affairs that India was crippled by its inability to deploy SF in an offensive role i.e. cross-border. Yet, I remember playing golf with a colonel in the army aviation and saying to him, "I suppose you people are trying hard to get night-flying capability." "No", he said. Perplexed, I asked, "I suppose you have a case for operating medium-lift helicopters integrated with SF as your first priority?" "No", he said. I suppose someone in army headquarters is trying desperately to give the SF a night insertion capability," I persisted. He again said, "No". This conversation has been repeated many times with others. This gives me the clear impression that the level of strategic thinking inside the AAC is underdeveloped and still in its infancy.

The AAC case seems to be to tell the government, "if you give us more money we will grow bigger and have bigger helicopters and be able to do more." This doesn't sound to me like a strategy. I haven't seen it stated anywhere that if the army aviation gets the helicopters it needs, the country will have a cross-border SF capability -or that the strike corps will have double the penetration capability that it now has, and how the nature of warfare either in the desert or the mountains or the jungles will change, thereby affecting the country's grand strategy. This is a big gap which the army aviation officers seem untrained to fill. ■

Army Aviation Structures in USA, UK, France and Germany: Evolution, Importance, Roles and Major Air Assets

— Brigadier Devinder Singh

Introduction

An examination of army aviation structures to include their evolution, importance, roles and major air assets of four major countries is a lengthy affair. It is therefore proposed to focus mainly on the army aviation of the US and to some extent that of UK. Army aviation structures of France and Germany are almost similar to that of UK. Keeping in view the objectives of formulating Vision: 2025 for the Indian Army Aviation, the endeavour will be to minimise the rudimentary details but highlight certain conceptual and evolutionary benchmarks and other salient features of army aviation in these countries from which we can draw relevant lessons.

US Army Aviation

The birth of aviation in the US Army was way back in 1909 and interestingly it was in the Corps of Signals which adopted this novel idea for ensuring speedy delivery of mail. In 1912, US Artillery started using aircrafts for spotter tasks. Modern army aviation came into being on June 6, 1942; a few months after the US entered World War II. To distinguish it from the air force (then known as army air force), it was called 'Organic Army Aviation'. Though its primary function was the adjustment of artillery fire, its small fixed-wing aircrafts (also known as Grasshoppers) came to be increasingly used for combat support and combat service support. In 1947, the army air force became the USAF and army aviation acquired its first helicopter. Incidentally this acquisition was much later than the air force, navy or even the coast guard got their helicopters.

In the early stages the US Army was allegedly encumbered by the restrictive approach adopted by the USAF which even controlled the nature of equipment to be acquired by the army aviation. This 'turf' battle between the

US Army and the USAF is well documented and had its share of 'anecdotal' bloomers. For example in the early 1950s, the US Army's quest for enhancing its tactical air mobility was rebuffed by the then director of USAF with the following cryptic remarks: -

"I am the Director of Requirements and I will determine what is needed and what is not. The helicopter is aerodynamically unsound. It is like lifting oneself by one's bootstraps. It is no good as an air vehicle and I am not going to procure any. No matter what the Army says. I know what it needs and what it does not."

(in reply to a request by Major General James M. Gavin of US Army.)

Notwithstanding such spats and thanks primarily to civilian foresight and intervention, what then followed was a series of negotiations and agreements wherein the areas of dispute between the army and the air force were gradually resolved over the next decade or so. It culminated into Johnson-McConnell Agreement of April 6, 1966, which authorised the army to freely develop and employ rotary-wing craft of all sizes for all intra-theatre purposes, including troop movement and fire support. In return, army aviation gave up any claim on larger fixed-wing aircraft and became more of a rotary-wing force. From 1966 onwards, the US Army became the nodal agency or recognised leader for helicopter development and related weapons, tactics and doctrine. As the airland battle concept progressed, another landmark agreement was signed in 1984, called the '31 Initiatives', which ensured jointness between the army and the air force in battlefield interdiction.

1966 was 40 years ago. Drawing a parallel in our context, only the observation and utility helicopters were integrated into the army 20 years ago in 1986. When and in what form will the balance of rotary assets be transferred to the army aviation cannot remain a closed subject and merits active consideration.

Evolution, change and development in the US Army Aviation was also enabled by other 'drivers', such as the unique and structured nature of the security apparatus in the US, which lends itself to continuous development, refinement and accountability. For example in 1962, 11th Air Assault Test Division was fielded to test the concept of tactical air mobility for the army, under the aegis of the defence secretary. More of this later. In addition, certain circumstantial landmarks did occur which shaped the US Army Aviation to its present state. These catalytic events were the Korean and Vietnam Wars, the Cold War, collapse of the Soviet Union/ Warsaw Pact and the Global war on Terrorism (GWOT). Each of these events impacted singularly on the force structure and employment of US Army Aviation as under: -

- **Korean and Vietnam Wars.** Lessons of the Korean War and developments in early 1960s under the initiative of President Kennedy and Defence Secretary McNamara led to a restructuring programme for the US Army known as the 'Reorganised Objectives Army Division' (ROAD). In 1962, it was immediately followed by the 'Howze Board'. Both these programmes recognised that transition of the army to air mobility was inevitable, just as it was in the past from animal mobility to motor mobility. The moot question was, what and how much constitutes air mobility- a lift capability of a company/ battalion/ brigade or more per division? The Howze Board recommended creation of five air assault divisions in an army which had 16 divisions then i.e. almost one-third of the entire army. The proposed structure of the then airborne brigade, in pursuit of tactical air mobility concept, simply replaced each motor vehicle with a helicopter. Notwithstanding above, it enabled the raising of air mobile divisions, wherein the 1st Cavalry Division (Air Mobile) was fielded in the Vietnam War in mid-1965 (and later became equipped with the turbine engined UH-1 (Huey). Two years later, 101st Airborne Division was also deployed bringing the number of army helicopters in Vietnam to a mammoth figure of above 3,500. The substantial role played by the army aviation in this war was widely acknowledged. Also a new breed of armed helicopters AH-1 (Cobra) was fielded and became an essential component for providing direct fire support. The helicopter had graduated from a concept of 'battle-taxi' to a 'combatised' role.
- **Cold War.** During the period of 1970-80s, in the changed environment of NATO-Warsaw Pact standoff in Europe, a doctrinal change was warranted. A reorganisation of the US Army titled as the 'Army of Excellence' Force Design (AOE), was initiated, with emphasis on specially designed 'attack helicopters' and 'armed scouts' operating together in flying NOE/ night time environment in mid to high intensity conventional operations. It brought in tailor- made organisations with mission related units i.e. attack battalions, cavalry squadrons, assault and command companies and medium- lift helicopter companies. Since it catered for an 'All Out War', it was even more ambitious than the Vietnam experience in the number of formations fielded (or those held in reserve) and hence in the number of helicopters required. The US Army then comprised of four corps headquarters, 10 active divisions and four to eight reserve divisions, apart from two armoured cavalry regiments. The aviation formations are integral to theatre commands, corps, air assault

division, airborne/ armoured/ mechanised/ light divisions. Outline organisation and aviation assets of aviation brigades of various types of divisions are at Appendix. This large scale expansion also led to the acceptance of aviation as a separate branch in April 1983, along with its separate cadre. However, large voids prevailed in the envisaged organisations, manpower and equipment holding except in the high priority formations.

- **Post-Cold War.** With the collapse of the Soviet Union in 1991 and thereby the Warsaw Pact, the main 'enemy' for the US Army suddenly disappeared. The need of large corps and army-sized formations to operate against massed tanks and other armoured vehicles was no longer there. Accordingly, the US Army in 1993 adopted the 'Aviation Restructure Initiative' (ARI). Understandably, it drastically reduced the number of attack helicopters at the corps level, undertook rationalisation of voids and pushed down specialised heliborne capabilities to the divisional level. Lessons from Operation Desert Storm (1991), though mainly related to maintenance, also contributed to these reforms. A comparative table showing the drastic reduction, especially in attack helicopters is shown below.

Table 1: Cold War and Post-Cold War US Army Aviation Assets.

	Attack	Scout	Utility	Cargo	Total*
AOE**	930	1,930	2,530	520	5910
ARI***	560	1,310	2,100	460	4430
(-)	370	620	430	60	1480

* Figures also include armed helicopters.

- **GWOT.** Post 9/11, a need was felt for global military presence with rapid deployment capability to counter terrorism involving possible intervention by the US. This also signalled the ultimate death-blow to a purely anti-tank helicopter and initiated a professional shift to a multi-purpose strike helicopter. The Afghanistan experience revealed the other shortcomings of US Army Aviation in deployability, survivability and sustainability. There were also the problems of high-altitude, multi-agency jointnesss in operations and integration of the newly introduced UAVs and unmanned combat aircrafts. It is revealing that though a high-readiness formation, 101st Airborne Division was the last to be fielded in Afghanistan primarily due to its unwieldiness, transportation difficulties and the need for vast infrastructure support. Marines, naval aviation being ship-based and even the air force operating from the occupied airfields, reached and commenced out of area (OOA) operations much earlier than the army aviation. Accordingly, a study was undertaken and a major restructuring and revitalisation of US Army Aviation is presently underway to overcome these shortcomings and make the army aviation more readily usable and capability oriented. A large number of these drawbacks were overcome in time for the invasion of Iraq.

Reviews and Modernisation Plans

In the last 25 years, 17 reviews of army aviation have been undertaken. Most of these reviews were overlapping and at times contradictory, but having been dictated by the events, technology and finances were largely relevant and proved to be good catalysts. For example, the 'Commanche' helicopter development programme (for a state-of-the-art deep penetration attack helicopter) undertaken near the end of the Cold War (1987-88) has recently been shelved in view of its marginal utility in a changed security environment, in spite of seven billion dollars having been already spent on its development. Aviation is a costly business and projections once made have long-term implications. In our context a formalised, high-powered and accountable reviewing organisation for the army aviation will be essential to monitor and make mid-course corrections where necessary. It may be best to encourage civilian involvement in research and development and manufacture of aviation assets, as within the armed forces, aviation is a small branch and that will find difficulty in competing with the old and well entrenched interests and lobbies, all by itself.

UK Army Air Corps

Very early in the World War II, the RAF under tremendous pressure during Dunkirk and the Battle of Britain realised that the concept of army co-operation squadrons thus far provided by the RAF was not sustainable and that the army would have to cater for its own aviation support. The army observation squadrons were then raised and in 1942, army aviation came into being. It comprised of the Air OP Squadrons, the Parachute Regiment and the Glider Pilots Regiment. However, they remained under the air ministry up till September 1957, when they were transferred to the war office and the Army Air Corps was thus founded. In 1970, it became an autonomous branch within the army, under the General Staff Branch. In 1999, the JHC was established to control all battlefield helicopters owned by the three services, being essential assets in the new strategic environment and to support all UK defence missions and tasks. The concept may hold lessons for us and needs to be debated. Simulation studies and experience during the Cold War revealed that the ratio of tank kills achieved by the helicopters was much higher than any other weapon system. This enabled its recognition as a combat arm.

• The JHC

- **Air Assets.** The air assets available to army aviation are its 300 or more helicopters and 30 fixed-wing aircrafts.
- **The Role.**
- * To deliver and sustain effectively battlefield helicopters and other air assault assets.
- * To be operationally capable under all environmental conditions to support all defence missions of the UK.
- **The Organisation.** The organisation is appended below.

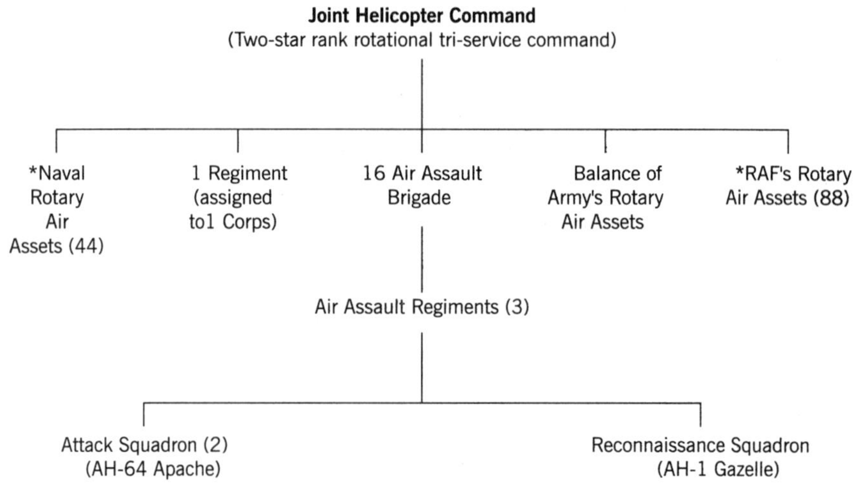

*This excludes RAF's search and rescue and Royal Navy's air early warning, anti-submarine and search and rescue rotary air assets.

Fig. 1: Organisation of Joint Helicopter Command (UK)

As stated earlier the suitability of a JHC in the Indian context needs evaluation. In fact, such a concept could even be extrapolated for another similar organisation to control all transport and communication aircrafts of the three services.

France

French Army Aviation was established on November 22, 1954. The major element of the French Army Aviation is its airmobile brigade. The organisation of the airmobile brigade is given below.

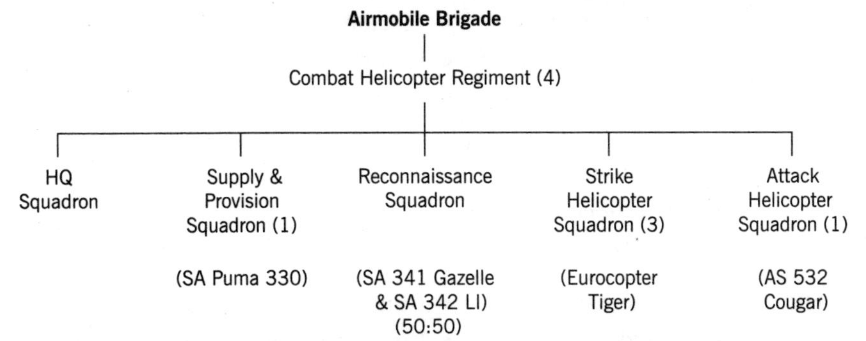

Fig. 2: Organisation of French Airmobile Brigade.

Germany

German Army Aviation was disbanded after World War II and re-established in 1957 in the then Federal Republic of Germany. Presently, the army aviation consists of four transport regiments, two attack regiments and two liaison squadrons. The inventory of helicopters in the German Army is 302 attack/ armed helicopters, 322 light/ medium utility helicopters and 42 other types -a total of 666 flying machines.

Role and Tasks

Apart from semantics, the role and tasks of army aviation of these countries are generally common in nature. The exception is the 'Cavalry' unit/ formation concept of US Army Aviation which involves a 'All Arms Command' of both ground and air combat elements. Another interesting factor is that UK, France and Germany, in spite of limited resources, have concentrated their aviation resources and have at least one aviation brigade each. This is not the case in India, even though the number of helicopters held by the army is reasonable. Should we get another 100 or more helicopters, will we (as an academic exercise) raise an aviation formation or distribute them to supplement the helicopter resources of our numerous formations? Unless a thought is given, the latter will be the obvious option. Primary, secondary and miscellaneous roles assigned to the army aviation of the USA, UK, France and Germany are appended below:-

Table 2: Army Aviation Roles in USA, UK, France and Germany.

Country	Primary	Secondary	Miscellaneous
USA	• Destroy enemy forces by fire and move and shock effect in support of offensive/ defensive operations. • Reconnaissance operations.	• Provide security. • Deep operations. • Liaison. • Command and control.	• ELINT & SIGINT • Cas evac.
UK	• Attack tasks. • Armed reconnaissance. • Security tasks.	• Control of fire. • Communication. • Command and control	• Cas evac. • Resupply. • Recovery.
France	• Reconnaissance operations. • Assault. • Supply.	• Special operations. • Communication	• Cas evac.
Germany	• Attack tasks. • Armed reconnaissance.	• Provide security. • Liaison. • Resupply.	• Cas evac.

Relevance in the Indian Context

In a changed security environment, where the probability of 'All Out Wars' and high intensity tank battles has comparatively decreased, whereas probability of localised skirmishes in high-altitude area/ OOTW/ OOA operations has become very high. We need pragmatism in understanding and dealing with this change. While there is a need to optimally manage the existing threats, (which will continue to persist), there is also a simultaneous, if not greater need to build capabilities to exploit the arising opportunities to further national interests and stature. In this, tactical air mobility of the army (provided mainly by army aviation) is a prime ingredient and needs to be akin to other modern armies of the world, with whom we are either co-operating or we support.

We see daily headlines in most newspapers talking of 120 new multi-role combat aircraft for air force, aircraft carrier and nuclear submarine for the navy, upgrade for the infantry and guns for the artillery and so on. But one fails to see any mention of or a debate on army aviation. The current 'incremental path' being taken by the army aviation is likely to yield only marginal results. Lessons need to be learnt from the US experience and a debate be initiated for acquiring air mobility capability for the army in both tactical as well as in the strategic arena, which will bring in substantial upgrades for army aviation. It will be simultaneously essential to build in national interest and services' consensus in this regard.

Lessons and Suggested Measures

Given the traditional impediments faced by other armies in democratic countries in expanding their army aviation, our problems are even greater because of a comparative lack of civilian interest in any debate on defence. Some lessons in this regard are drawn from the evolution of the US and European army aviation:-

- **Propagation of a Concept of Air Mobility for the Army.** The Indian Army has since graduated from being 'animal transport' based, to being 'mechanical transport' based. It is time, that we catch up with the other armies and graduate, if only partially, to become 'airmobile'. The US began this transition way back in 1965, when they fielded their first airmobile division. Thirty years hence, Indian Army with its current capability and equipment profile will not be considered at par with other armies,'. If it does not develop on the lines of 'air-mobility' concept. Such an exercise will not only need substantial funding but also a change of mindset in the higher defence management arena. It would thus need formal propagation in the armed forces and in the public domain. Once the concept and requirement is well accepted, resource allocation will be easier.
- **Enhancing Civilian Interest in Army's Air-Mobility Concept.** Civilian interest and stakes, whether these are political, bureaucratic, public sector and private sector, need to be encouraged to participate, if army aviation is to expand in a substantial manner. It is their 'lobbying' that will lend the necessary impetus in overcoming the current impediments restricting the

growth of army aviation. It is of interest to note that in the US, the political, bureaucratic and the business circles, relate all rotary-wing aircraft (including their future development) with the army and not the USAF.

- **Interim Measures for Jointness.** Without prejudice to any long term arrangements that may emerge in our context between the army, air force and the navy, the following measures in the interim are suggested to enhance jointness:-
  - **Macro Level.** Notwithstanding the vested interests of respective services, there is a need to consider creation of JHC and a 'Joint Transport Aircraft Command'. The army could 'head' the 'JHC', whereas air force could 'head' the 'Joint Transport Aircraft Command'. This would go a long way in easing the 'turf' battle between the services.
  - **Functional Level.** An aviation brigade needs to be raised for each operational command of the army. These brigades will be composite in nature having Weapon Support Integrated (WSI), Utility and Tactical Battle Support (TBS) units on their orbat. They would further have under their operational control; not only the attack helicopters of the air force (which presently are under the army's operational control) but also most of the medium lift helicopter units of the air force. This would essentially aim to give 'one company lift' capability to each operational command of the Indian Army. Though such an arrangement falls short of the army's long-term projection of these assets being part of the AAC, such a measure in an immediate time frame will go a long way in ensuring the requisite integrated training for attack helicopter and heliborne operations, which is thus far lacking.
  - **Choice of Combat Helicopter.** Given the escalating cost factor and the changing nature of war, wherein mechanised operations are going to be limited, a multi-role helicopter should be preferred over a dedicated 'attack helicopter' as a weapon platform for induction into the army aviation. The 'attack helicopter' is too 'limited' in its role and other parameters. This lesson was well driven home in the Kargil War when these helicopters could not be used. A multi-role helicopter would be better suited to provide the necessary flexibility for such varied employment. ■

Organisation of US Army Aviation Formations

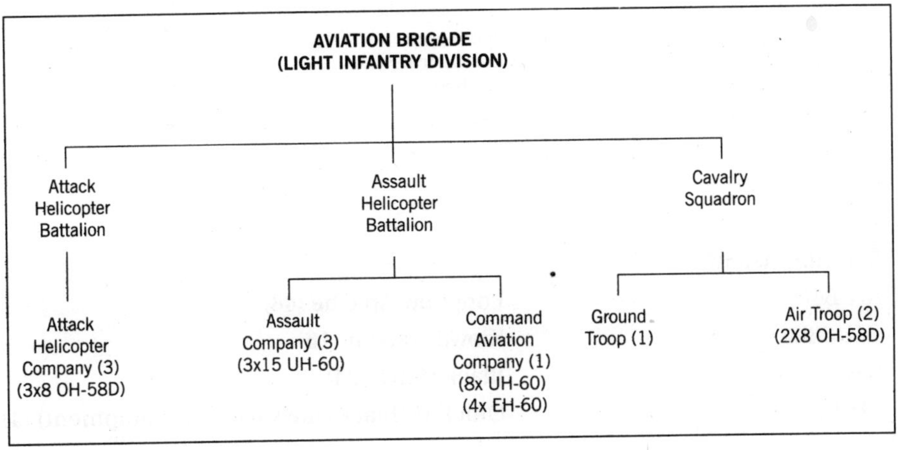

Aviation Assets:

OH-58D	-	Kiowa Warrior (40)
UH-60	-	Black Hawk (53)
EH-60	-	Quickfix (Black Hawk with EW equipment) (4)

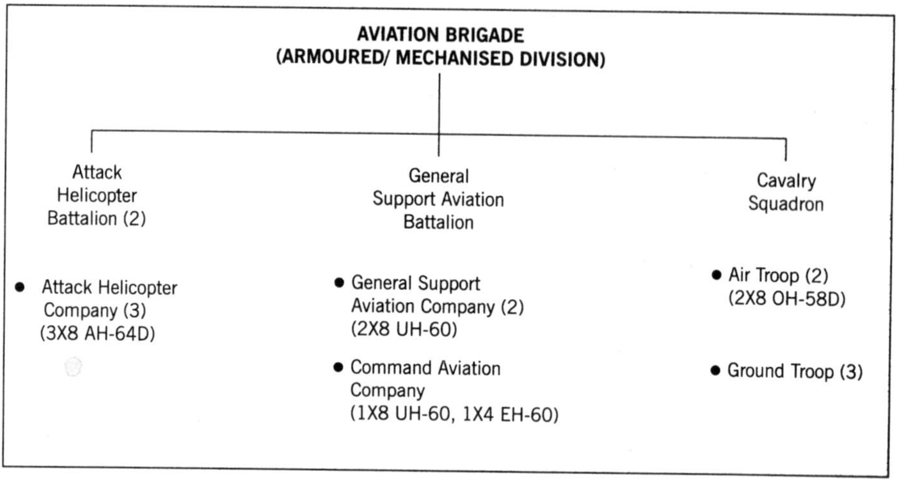

Aviation Assets:

AH-64D	-	Longbow Apache (48)
OH-58D	-	Kiowa Warrior (16)
UH-60	-	Black Hawk (24)
EH-60	-	Quickfix (Black Hawk with EW equipment) (4)

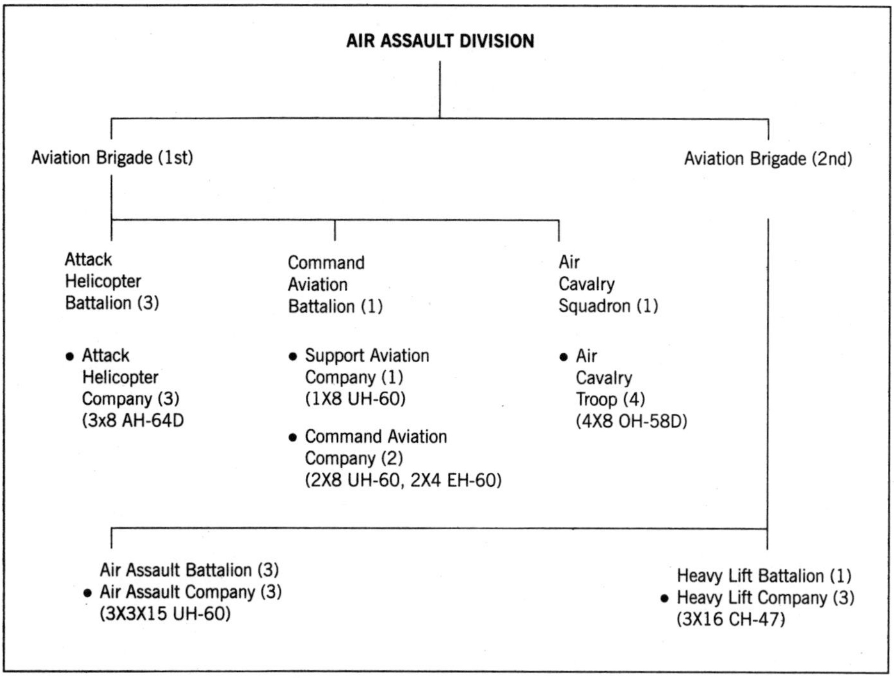

Aviation Assets:

AH-64D	-	Longbow Apache (72)
OH-58D	-	Kiowa Warrior (16)
UH-60	-	Black Hawk (159)
EH-60	-	Quickfix (Black Hawk with EW equipment) (8)
CH-47	-	Chinook (48)

Army Aviation Structures in Israel, Russia, China and Pakistan

— Lieutenant General G. S. Sihota

Introduction

A study of evolution, importance, roles and major assets of important armies of the world can provide good inputs for restructuring India's Army Aviation. An analysis of their doctrines and force structures may lead us to a road map suitable for meeting the needs of our defence forces.

We have chosen to analyse the growth and employment of the army aviation of the USA (sole superpower) and other European countries, with immense experience in utilisation of air power. Similarly, study of Russian aviation is important as the Soviet Union was the other superpower till recently and continues to maintain large defence forces. In fact, correct lessons can only be drawn by the study of the erstwhile Soviet Union. Israeli Defence Forces (IDF) are comparatively younger but are the most experienced, having fought four major wars in a short span of time and are continuously engaged in anti-terrorist operations and LIC. The importance of two of our immediate neighbours i.e. Pakistan and China cannot be ignored, as their capabilities affect our own force structure and tactics.

Some of these countries have AACs, which are an offshoot of their air forces, whereas others have carved their air force from the army aviation assets. Some nations having felt the need to integrate the aviation requirement of the land forces with their armies have achieved it by retaining a tactical air force as part of the air force, but have ensured its full integration with the army during training and actual operations. The command and control structure of these has been fine-tuned accordingly. Therefore correct lessons can be drawn by not only studying the army aviation per se but by studying the role of air power in providing support to the land forces and the philosophy being adopted to integrate this effort.

Each of these countries have utilised its own experience and incorporated lessons of various campaigns and battles of other countries. The employment of helicopters needs special attention, as they are becoming more and more useful in combat and combat support operations in future.

For creating a new structure in the armed forces or for restructuring an existing one, we need to establish the necessity, convince the approving authorities of the futuristic needs, clear the way by preventing dissent by various rivals and arrange adequate funds and resources. Our study should reflect on the approach followed by these countries in tackling these issues and methods adopted by them to overcome such hurdles.

Israel

The Israel Army can perhaps provide maximum valid reasons for employment of air in support of land forces. A society which once had no soldiers became a nation of soldiers in the span of a single generation. In 1973, it sent into battle the third largest tank force and the sixth largest air force in the western world.

Its army grew through trial and error and through experimentation and debate. Israelis have taught themselves, virtually everything they know, from basic infantry skills to the intricacies of air combat. The army's doctrines, tactics and structures are the original creation of the Israelis themselves. That perhaps is the strongest reason for us to study their growth and methods.

Israeli Army's doctrine is to prepare for a short duration war, place reliance on offensive strategy and achieve air superiority to cover the move of forces on the ground. They contend that air support and reconnaissance are more important for security of mobile columns engaged in offensive operations than for static forces holding defensive positions.

Till 1948, the army remained essentially an infantry force. On May 26, 1949 the provisional government ordered for establishment of the IDF consisting of ground, naval and air forces.

It is to be noted that Israeli Air Force (IAF) is not a separate service but a corps of a single service -Army; even though it has its distinctive uniform, maintains its own specialised services and has an operational headquarters. This semi-autonomous status was a result of a compromise between the advocates of full integration with the land forces and for an independent status to air force as a separate service.

During the war of Independence in 1947-49, air force had a modest beginning with a few aircrafts mainly barrowed, stolen and refurbished. The air force lacked scale of priorities with which to choose between different combat missions; neither did it have a tactical doctrine which fitted the needs of the ground forces. Few available combat aircraft were used for poorly co-ordinated missions in the enemy's rear, at the expense of close support for the forces on the ground. Effective co-operation with the ground forces was the exception rather than the rule.

Till 1953, the Chief of Staff of IDF was chosen from the ground forces and was responsible for all operations. Air and naval units had only functional autonomy. Both IAF and the Israel Navy maintained own country-wide operational headquarters, co-operating with and not under the control of area commanders of land force.

Though, inter-services relations were cordial, initially, major challenge to the unity of IDF came from the IAF. Aspiring to an independent status, IAF's 27-year-old Commander, Ashron Remez asserted that air force is not an auxiliary service of the ground forces. He claimed that air superiority will decide the battle and air force is a decisive force. He demanded total independence and preferential treatment for his airmen in promotions, pay and housing. Yadin who was the Chief of Staff refused to consider it. The defence minister (Gunon) tried to mediate a compromise but failed and finally Remez was removed from his post in mid-1950. By 1951, there were only 5,000 soldiers in the IAF and Navy, supporting a land force of 11 brigades.

It could be claimed that the Arab-Israel theatre of war was basically continental. That is to say, its decisive battles would be fought on land. Having recognised this aspect, when economic limitations compelled Israel to observe strict priorities in the matter of expenditure, the land force with their air support was given first priority. It was for this reason, along with the desire to avoid inter-service rivalry and waste, and to achieve maximum co-operation, efficiency and coherence that all armed services with their particular commanders were placed under a single central staff headed by an army general.

After Ashron, Chaim Laskov, a ground leader was appointed commander of the IAF. It was he who developed a new combat doctrine suggesting employment of mobile armour units supported by air power. It also laid the foundation for converting the IAF from propeller to a jet air force.

One of the major lessons of the Sinai campaign was the need for expansion of armour and air power and their integration. IAF was prevented from opening the campaign with a classical strike against the Egyptian Air Force on the ground. Instead, limited air force was employed for covering the ground attack by establishing control over the battle area, interdict hostile movements and provide close ground support.

From Sinai to Six Days War in 1967, Israelis divided their air force entities, high performance machines into air superiority fighter and slower and less costly ones for ground support and attack role.

Israel's opponents were mainly guided by Russian doctrines and methods of warfare: mass concentration of tanks and long-range artillery closely supported by tactical air force. To meet this challenge Israelis placed greater stress on development of land forces particularly armour closely supported by air force. The infantry brigade remained the biggest tactical unit; a number of operational commands were created, each incorporating several brigades. This new type of command could perhaps be described as a very large task force (in Hebrew, *Ugda*) similar to a division.

In the development of air capabilities, Israelis did not concentrate on strategic air force at the cost of land forces, which was considered more important. On the other hand efficient tactical air force was considered vital.

Despite the emphasis on land forces, it was the IAF, which laid the foundation of Israel's victory on June 5, 1967 by destroying the air potential of its enemy in a few hours. It gambled on first strike, committing practically all of its first line combat aircrafts. If the surprise had failed and if the enemy had managed to intercept the heavily loaded aircrafts there might have been serious losses.

The winning combination of 1967 war i.e. armour and air power led Israel concentrating on development of a new doctrine and expansion of a complimentary force structure. As a result of this modernisation, infantry and artillery and basic night-fighting tactics got neglected. There was some criticism of this approach.

After 1967, the tendency to underestimate the air force was replaced by the opposite. Many came to see in the IAF, an all-purpose force, which could achieve any and all goals. In the next four years, Israelis were to receive full education on limitations of air power.

In their criticism many had observed that heavy German bombardment of the British Isles during World War II had not subdued Britain. Similarly, heavy American bombardment of North Vietnam had not broken its people's will to fight. One has to conclude that until one side's territory is occupied and land forces break the resistance of it's people and it's army, no war comes to an end unless, indeed it is brought to an end by a peaceful settlement.

By 1973, when Yom Kippur War took place, it was felt that IDF were neither well-balanced, nor integrated and lacked combined arms doctrine.

It can be seen that in 1956, the role of IAF was limited to close support of the ground forces, interdiction strikes against enemy communications in the rear and battlefield air cover. In 1956, Egyptians suffered heavy casualties from Israeli air attacks especially at Sham el-sheikh, when the air force acted in direct support of ground forces. In 1967, IAF was given a central role. The situation got reversed after 1973 due to the shortcomings noticed in the war of Atonement. The air force did not enter the war according to plan and had to fight against very heavy odds. The IAF had prepared for this conflict on the assumption that at the outbreak of hostilities it would be given adequate time to concentrate on the missile threat, without being involved in interdiction or close support in the first phase. Apart from the defence of Israeli airspace, the air force was to enjoy certain latitude without being obliged to care for the ground forces. This was a grave mistake. When Egyptians swarmed the Suez Canal defences, air force had to be committed to close support role, for which it was ill-prepared and had to meet heavy demand for the close support pouring in from all along the front. The Egyptians and Syrians, on the other hand, concentrated their air effort to provide close support to their troops in the general area of the front line. Day by day air warfare is becoming highly involved and complicated affair. To a degree, air power will obviously not be as influential as it has been and will affect the battlefield less than it did. The proliferation of light, portable missile launchers in the front line means that close support by the air force will be the exception to the rule in the future, with the air force being obliged to concentrate on isolating the battlefield, maintaining supremacy in the area and destroying the rear of the battlefield. The close support tasks will have to be managed by the army through close integration of such air resources with the land forces.

In 1967, at the Battle of Um Katef, Ariel Sharon had demonstrated that a precise orchestration of fire and move between infantry, tanks, artillery and heliborne troops was possible on a divisional scale and at night.

Now, Israelis are following a balanced approach, as swift military victory is unthinkable without air superiority and integration of resources with ground forces for close air support is considered essential. Accordingly, they have undertaken expansion of the tactical air force which can give close support to rapidly advancing land forces; also perform additional tasks such as surveillance, EW, transportation and landing of troops (including paratroopers) communications, ambulance work and rescue operations.

Helicopters have found a special place in the Israeli Army's inventory. First squadron was inducted in the Sixties. Six Day's War marked the first large-scale appearance of helicopters in the field. Now attack helicopters are being used extensively, including for counter-terrorism operations.

Russia

When one talks about the Russian armed forces, one is in fact referring to erstwhile Soviet Union. There are striking dissimilarities between the Soviet and the western concepts of employment of air power. Soviet military doctrine shapes the organisation, equipment and employment of air force, as well as employment of air in support of ground operations. Many factors have combined to produce this particular way of warfare. These include Russian (as distinctive from Soviets) character, environment and national consciousness.

Soviet armed forces were tailored to operate over the vast expanse of Soviet territory which has been the battleground of Soviet Imperial Russian Armies for centuries.

The Soviet air power has always remained in the shadow of the land forces. The tactical air force of the frontal aviation (*Frontovaya Aviatsiya*) has formed the Soviet Air Force, whose employment and operations have been rigidly subordinated to those of the land armies.

Until the major reorganisation of 1980s, each Soviet land army had its own air army and since that time the land and the air forces have been even more closely integrated. Although, air force is an independent service but its major preoccupation is the support of ground operations. There is no strong Soviet tradition of independent air operations, as it exists in the USAF or the RAF.

The most frequently stressed military dictum in Soviet defence literature is perhaps the primacy of offensive action. If the Soviet armed forces had to go to war, the aim would be a swift and overwhelming victory over enemy forces. Decisive conventional victory is to be achieved before nuclear weapons come into play. They believe in penetrating into enemy defensive positions and intermingling with the defender, thus offering a poor target for the defender. High speed and momentum of advance is the key to success. All available forces must be co-opted, demanding extremely close co-ordination of ground and air action. Tactical air force had become much more closely integrated with the ground forces being supported.

Command and control had been accordingly structured. At theatre level, each commander-in-chief (C-in-C) of theatre of operations had a deputy commander from frontal aviation. Similarly, at lower level the army commander of 16 military districts and four groups of Soviet forces had deputy commanders from tactical aviation.

Battlefield support helicopters in Soviet era were part of air force organisation. Helicopters were employed for land troops to reinforce the artillery, which had moved forward and to ensure its security by landing armed troops. Helicopters worked very closely with the ground troops. An aviation division organisation had a divisional headquarters, three air regiments and an independent squadron entrusted with reconnaissance and transport tasks. Each air regiment had three air squadrons.

Heliborne assault troops in battalion or brigade strength are used effectively to force through the depth of enemy's deployment, co-ordinate raids over rear areas with frontal assault to achieve maximum disruption and damage to material and morale.

Soviet Army was comparatively late in seeing advantage to be gained in tactical mobility through helicopter airlift. In 1960, when USA was conducting airmobile helicopter operations in Vietnam, Soviets had no comparable capability.

However, they could see a new potential for helicopters. In 1974, Mi-24 Hind transport gunship was introduced. It revolutionised the helicopter warfare. Now their Mi-6 can lift a tractor under slung. During the Ethiopian War in 1978, imaginative employment of helicopters was observed during the Battle of Jgjiga. Soviets used the helicopters to lift men and armoured vehicles over a mountain barrier to take the Somali defenders in the rear. From then on, Soviets increased their strength of some 400 tactical helicopters to double within five years.

Soviets also found that helicopters were most effective weapon in CI operations in Afghanistan. Though the helicopters were part of air force's frontal aviation command and not an independent army's air arm; but the distinction was largely academic one, as the integration between helicopter forces and the army was close.

Large strength of Soviet helicopters was divided into functional categories as follows:-

- Mi-24 Hind- Assault Transport and Attack Role. - 800
- Mi-8 Hip-Assault Transport. - 1500
- Mi-6-Hook Cargo Transport. - 400
- Mi-26 Halo- Heavy Lift.
- Mi-I
Mi-II
Mi-IV } For miscellaneous duties. - 750

Although the primary reason for the growth of frontal aviation's combat helicopter units in the late 70s was undoubtedly to increase tactical mobility of ground units; one outcome of this expansion has been to provide the army with a new form of fire support -the armed attack helicopter.

The attack helicopter was an innovation of the Vietnam War and was originally intended to provide fire support and armed escort for troop carrying helicopters. It was found that a specialised attack helicopter was needed to bring down suppressive fire before and during landing operations, when the troop-carrying machines were most vulnerable to ground fire.

It is interesting to read that in Vietnam the USAF, was reluctant to allow the army's attack helicopters to develop their close air support potential to the full, as this trespassed on a jealously guarded air force's preserve. Soviets also observed that US Army's efforts to use aircrafts for greater tactical mobility were hampered by the partisans of the USAF, which had been divorced from the army by the Congress on July 26, 1947, by establishing a separate army aviation arm. Air force accused the army of duplicating its role.

Soviet articles on tactical problems of heliborne assaults certainly made reference to the American experience in Vietnam. It is perhaps not a coincidence that in 1967, the year when AH-1 attack helicopter went into action in Vietnam, the Soviet Air Force experimented with armed helicopters' in exercise "*Dnepr*". However, it is likely that the helicopter attack missions were regarded as secondary to its trooping duties. That is the reason that Mi-24 D&E specialised attack helicopters still retain the capacity to carry a squad of infantry.

Soviet senior generals have gone so far as to claim that vertical envelopment of the enemy has become an important manoeuvre without which not a single contemporary offensive operation will be possible. Helicopters can be used as alternative to air strikes to knock out enemy headquarters, airfields, radars, communication equipments and nuclear weapons and delivery systems. These, of course, comprise the overriding priority objectives for all Soviets.

Soviets had airlift capability of seven divisions. The Soviet Army had accordingly formed eight airmobile brigades. Airmobile brigades were assigned to theatre commanders, whereas airmobile divisions were directly controlled by the Soviet high command. Military transport aviation has a capability for tactical transport with IL-76 and AN-12, heavy transport with AN-22, troop transport with IL-16, utility transport with AN-26 and VIP transport with IL-26, TU-134, TU-154 and Yak-40.

China

Since the foundation of communist regime in Peking in 1949, China's military arm i.e. PLA has been involved in four conflicts i.e. invasion of Tibet in 1950, Korean War, conflict with India in 1962, armed confrontation with Soviet Union in 1969-73 and a border war with Vietnam. The PLA exercises overall command and control over all armed forces. The PLAAF functions directly under the Chief of General Staff of the General Staff Department of the PLA. In 1958, transfer of utility helicopters from the air force to the army, established PLA's Aviation Corps (PLAAC). The role of the AAC is to support ground troops as a transport force with the majority of its helicopter fleet being transport and utility machines.

Each group army, which is equivalent to a corps, has an army aviation regiment, eight such army aviation regiments operate under five helicopter brigades assigned to selected armies. These helicopter brigades when fully mobilised, typically operate from 84 to 245 machines. Each brigade controls one to three regular aviation regiments and two or more reserve units. AAC regiments normally have three squadrons which operate 8 to 12 machines.

While this represents a significant capability, when compared with USA and Russia, rotary-wing effort available to PLA units is modest. Certain rapid deployment force units are associated with specific aviation regiments for operations. The organisation appears logical as it permits selected group army commanders to control a critical resource.

Earlier, PLA's aviation regiments held and operated a single type of helicopter, but now newer equipment is being inducted on a squadron basis. Most of these squadrons have been equipped with transport helicopters, but having studied other armies of the world, attack helicopters are being inducted into the army.

The regular aviation regiments were originally equipped with MI-4, MI-8, Mi-17, SA/ AS-321 for heavy lift and AS-365 (Eurocopter) and WZ-9, which is China's gunship based on AS-365. China also has special units equipped entirely with WZ-9 in the Nanjing military region (MR).

Now, PLAAC also operate a single flight of AN-12 and has a VIP squadron with AS-332 and Bell-214 machines. It also has a heavy lift flight of MI-6s (alleged to have been stolen from shipment to Vietnam during the Vietnam War). All these detachments are subordinated to army aviation training unit located in the Beijing MR.

Since China has imported six different types of helicopters from different countries, it has caused logistics problem for their maintenance. Their own aviation industry is yet to produce a successful attack helicopter and a medium/ large transport helicopter. At present China has two helicopter manufacture complexes and a dedicated helicopter technique institute, but it can produce only around 40 machines every year.

Despite all this, AAC has developed limited combat capability with dozens of Harbin WZ-9 attack helicopters, eight Eurocopter AS-342E Gazelles and around 100 MI-17 Hip which are fitted with launchers to fire rockets and machine gun pods for ground attack roles. Chinese Army is considering enhancement of attack helicopter support in the near future.

The transport support now constitutes Z-9s, 24 Sikorsky S-70C, Black-Hawks, 60-plus Mi-17 Hip, and 3 Mi-6s. There are six Eurocopter AS-332 Super Pumas and a dozen of Mi-8 Hip, which have been inherited from the air force for VIP transportation and cas evac missions. In addition, some 30 to 40 AS-316, Alouette III and JHG Z-11s are available for training and communication role.

A summary of China's military helicopter fleet is as follows:-

Table 1: China's Military Helicopter Fleet

Model	Mission Role	Licensor	Number
Z-11	Training	JHG	12
MI-17/ 171	Transport, Ground Attack	Mil	60
MI-8	Passenger/Cargo/ Transport	Mil	(?)
S-70C	Transport	Sikorsky	24
Z-9A/B	Utility/ Transport	HAMC	80-100
Z-9C	ASW/ SAR	HAMC	(?)
AS-565	ASW/ SAR	Eurocopter	10-20
WZ-9	Attack- Anti-tank	HAMC	30 (+)
SA-342	Attack- Anti-tank	Eurocopter	6
Ka-28	ASW	Kamov	8-12
AS-332L	VIP Conveyance	Eurocopter	4
SA-316/ 318	Training	Eurocopter	(?)
Mi-6	Heavy Lift/ Transport	Mil	2-4

Pakistan

Pakistan Army Avation (PAA) gained autonomy from Pakistan Air Force in 1958, and attained the status of a full-fledged corps in 1977. Initially, Auster MK-5 and MK-6 were in service. In 1957, 60 O-1 Bird Dogs were delivered from the USA, which mostly replaced the Austers, thus making it possible to equip two frontline Air OP squadrons. More O-1s were later assembled at Army's 503 Workshop at Dhaimal, eventually producing 60 per cent of the components indigenously. The army also started the maintenance of its own aircrafts. In 1959, army aviation school was founded. 18 Bell 47/OH-13s were inducted in the army as soon as a batch of helicopter trained pilots returned from the USA in 1964. These aircraft allowed the formation of several composite units which were employed during the 1965 Indo-Pakistan War for spotting, liaison, and FAC tasks.

After the war, Pakistan acquired 24 Alouette IIIs from Aerospatiale of France; some of them were also assembled in Pakistan. Several other machines from different sources have joined these Alouettes, including six SA-315B Lamas from Romania in 1987. The Lamas are used for high-altitude operations in Siachin and Karakoram.

Medium–lift capability came with the procurement of 12 Mi-8s. These were used in rescue operations in East Pakistan, along with Alouette IIIs. Both these helicopters also saw some action during the war of 1971 in East Pakistan and were withdrawn from the theatre through Burma (Myanmar) before the capitulation of Pakistan Armed Forces.

In 1973, the US gifted six UH-1Hs for future disaster relief operations. In 1974, Iran donated 10 AB 205As. The same year 115 Saab MFI-17s were inducted for training and liaison; of these, 23 aircraft were supplied as complete aircraft and the rest in knocked down kit form which were to be assembled locally. These aircraft were named Mushak. Subsequently, Sweden transferred the production facility of this aircraft to Pakistan. In 1975, 12 Bell 206-Bs were acquired from USA, and a few Jet Rangers III joined them, a few years later.

In 1976, the army acquired 32 Aerospatiale SA-330J Pumas, which formed two new squadrons, and boosted the assault and medium-lift capability.

Pakistan Army's requirements for armed attack helicopters were fulfilled in 1985 when two squadrons, each with 10 AH-1S (Cobra), were raised. These squadrons also operate a few Bell 206-Bs as scout helicopters.

PAA's inventory of Mi-8s was doubled in 1997 when 12 Mi-17s were procured from the CIS. About half of these aircraft are located in Quetta. PAA also operates two Rockwell Turbo Commander fixed-wing aircrafts- a Commander MA Jetprop 840 for survey purpose and a Mc Donnell Douglous MD-500E for Inter Services Intelligence missions.

Organisation of PAA

The PAA's organisation has undergone a major change. It initially started with only aviation squadrons with limited support set up. Today, it has an aviation directorate, aviation command, aviation groups, training establishments and aviation bases.

The aviation directorate was raised in 1972 as part of the general headquarters (GHQ) and is headed by a major general. It is assessed that the aviation directorate would be responsible for training, equipment, documentation, policy formulation, publication and matters related to operations and administration.

The army aviation command was raised on August 6, 1986 at Rawalpindi and is commanded by a major general. It is responsible for exercising command and control over aviation groups, engineering and electrical and mechanical engineering (EME) battalions as well as (FAAR) companies.

In 2001-02, PAA raised five aviation groups (two each at Rawalpindi and Multan and one at Gujranwala). A brigadier commands each aviation group. PAA's 21 aviation squadrons have since been grouped with these aviation groups, which in all probability are responsible for their training and operational employment.

PAA squadrons are organised as under:-

- **Command Squadrons.** Two such squadrons exist and are equipped with AH-1S (Cobra) attack helicopters. Each squadron has nine attack, seven scout and five utility helicopters.
- **Composite Squadrons.** PAA has 12 composite squadrons and each squadron has three fixed-wing and a rotary-wing flight.
- **Utility Squadrons.** There are four utility squadrons each having two logistic and a utility flight.
- **Cargo Squadrons**. Three such squadrons exist, which are equipped with MI-8/ Puma helicopters. Each squadron has 10 Mi-8/ Puma and two light observation helicopters.

PAA has approximately 374 aircraft of all types in service, excluding the reserves. A summarised inventory is as under:-

• Attack Helicopters: AH-1S (Cobra)	-	18
• Medium-Lift Helicopters: (Mi-8 / Puma 330-L3)	-	34
• Light/ Medium-Lift Helicopters: (Lama/ Bell/ Alouette)	-	118
• Light Fixed-wing Aircrafts: (1-19/SAAB/MFI-17/Y)	-	204
Total:	-	**374**

Support base for PAA includes a base workshop, two engineering battalions, three EME battalions and three FAAR companies. Three aviation bases are responsible for all administrative support.

PAA is dependent on USA and other European countries for its aircrafts, spares, weapons and equipment. Its officers and men are trained in these countries and as such they are guided by the western concepts and tactics for the employment of the army aviation.

The question that is posed, "Should Indian AAC remain helicopter-based or add fixed-wing aircraft to its inventory and what role can be assigned to fixed-wing aircraft?" tends to ignore history and technology. ■

Optimising the Aviation Corps

— Air Commodore Jasjit Singh

As far as I remember, all aircraft with the aviation corps -when it was called the Air OP as its precursor were fixed-wing aircraft. These were light, essentially two-seater aircraft that also undertook the role of reconnaissance of the battlefield areas. It may be recalled that the British had come to an understanding, laying down an upper all-up-weight limit of aircraft that could be held by the army. It is instructive to remember that it was the experience of long-drawn World Wars that led to army leadership in the UK and the USA creating independent air forces in their countries. The only exceptions were the retention of Air OP tasks and capabilities with the army in view of the specialised nature of their missions. This was so in all countries and historically could be traced to World War I. Such aircraft could operate from short semi-prepared strips and hence were not dependent on prepared runways. Artillery ranges were comparatively limited and hence it was possible to undertake artillery spotting and fire correction by an airborne post in such aircraft even flying over enemy held territory. And, compared to later decades, battlefield anti-aircraft weaponry was primitive where it existed. Such aircraft naturally also could be used for communication duties at the disposal of the field formation commanders.

But what we need to recall is that the utility of such fixed-wing aircraft started to change with developments in technology. At one level, artillery ranges started to increase. Today tube-artillery with ranges of up to 40 km is fairly common in the inventories of most countries; and rocket-propelled artillery has even a longer reach. It is obvious that artillery spotting, fire correction etc. are simply outside the range of human observation even with high-powered optical aids and higher altitudes carry their own complexities and risks. Even more important fact is that in the battlefields evermore sophisticated and lethal anti-aircraft weaponry is making appearance. This drastically reduced the utility of the army aircraft close to the front line. But it was the advent of low-level radar cover in the battle zone that narrowed the usable operational envelope of the fixed-wing (as well as rotary-wing) aircraft in the battle zone, while increasing its vulnerability to ever increasing range, accuracy, lethality and density of anti-aircraft weaponry.

On the other hand, the invention and operationalisation of helicopters provided an alternate to the light fixed-wing aircraft. Their major advantage for close contact operations for artillery spotting and as FAC tasks (besides communications) was that they could take off, land, and hover in confined spaces. The NOE flying, with the ability to pop up, reconnoitre and fire weapons where required became crucial to avoiding enemy radar and anti-aircraft weaponry. Concurrently, developments of air-to-ground anti-tank guided missiles added an additional punch to the helicopters' capabilities to use firepower integral to it. As happened in the broader history of air power, battlefield tactical aircraft moved from pure reconnaissance and surveillance roles to include combat functions where finally even air-to-air combat and carriage of AAMs on helicopters became an important facet. NATO countries even designed tactical combat aircraft like the Alpha Jet to deal with what became a massive threat from Soviet helicopter force by ensuring tactical air superiority. With the increase in density of aviation and AD weaponry in the battle zone, serious problems of effective command and control of airspace started to emerge and the phenomenon of friendly fire continues to be acute. It was generally expected that in case of a shooting war between NATO and Warsaw Pact forces, as many as 33 per cent aircraft losses would be accounted for by friendly fire within the first 24 hours. On the face of it, therefore, it would appear to be a retrograde step to reverse history to bring back fixed-wing aircraft into army aviation role.

For a more detailed examination, the issue, therefore, requires an objective assessment of some of the key factors that influence it in various ways. Firstly, the macro trend in wars is toward expansion of the battle-space. This is due to a number of factors that we need not go into here. But what is clear is that range of weapons and their accuracy has been increasing necessitating lower force-to-space ratios compared to earlier periods. It also implies greater reliance on technology in every possible way to ensure accurate intelligence while keeping effective operational control over the battle-space and the combat forces involved. This development is accompanied specifically by the proliferation of densely deployed and highly accurate lethal AD weaponry of ever higher ranges which poses new threats to aircraft (fixed-wing as well as rotary-wing aircraft) in the battle zone.

At the same time, expanded battle-space also has led to an increasing degree of diffusion of the FLOT (Forward Line of Own Troops) and FLET (Forward Line of Enemy Troops). This is all the more significant in battles of manoeuvre where the fog of war itself tends to obliterate neat lines drawn on operational planning maps. While air power is more effective in manoeuvre warfare as compared to that in a static confrontation, such diffusion poses new risks of target identification and exposure of aircraft to ground fire since very often they would be forced to fly over hostile troops (regular and irregular).

While aircrafts are increasingly being equipped with defensive warning and counter-measure systems against missile and radar controlled AD guns, they remain highly vulnerable to small arms fire. Any advance over enemy territory runs the risk now of lethal small arms being used against low-flying (and inevitable slow speed intrinsic to army aviation assets) aircrafts. Helicopter attrition in Vietnam War provides enormous evidence of the vulnerability of helicopters in the battle zone even where the enemy does not possess sophisticated weaponry-or combat air power. In turn, the risks of friendly fire have also increased markedly. In specific, Iraq War demonstrated the vulnerability of low flying helicopters and aircraft to weapons like rocket-propelled grenade launchers and even assault rifles. It may recalled, that in a single mission, all the 30 US helicopters suffered sufficiently serious damage from such weapons for the mission to be abandoned. It does not require great imagination to assess the outcome if an enemy combat air power was also active in the area. Light fixed-wing slow flying aircraft would be inevitably more vulnerable due to their limitations of manoeuvrability compared to helicopters. No wonder no military now holds such aircraft in the inventories for battle zone employment.

A serious examination of the impact of expansion of the battle-space would indicate that this expansion restricts rather than increases the role of battlefield air power. Co-ordination of air and ground operations has become extremely complex. The greatest limitation is the challenge of effective command and control of airspace which must perforce be also used by high-speed combat aircraft operating in the area as well as transiting through the airspace above the battle zone at low altitude. High density of guided and unguided surface-to-air weaponry with ground forces poses serious challenge to air power operating at low-levels. While use of friendly battlefield radars would help in better air-space management, it also must be assumed that they would be the primary target for hostile air power for early suppression of AD weapons.

Secondly, in our context, we need to be clear what sort of war India would have to fight in the next two decades? It is generally agreed that such a war would be heavily influenced by the nuclear weapons factor. On the face of it, a short duration high-intensity war is much more likely to raise serious risk of escalation to a nuclear threshold. A full spectrum war with full spectrum capabilities would run a serious risk of destabilising the enemy leadership's perceptions and objectivity thus, lowering the threshold for a nuclear threat. Concepts like large-scale division level air assault forces against an enemy with a reasonably professional military and a capable hostile air power are no longer valid especially where the enemy also has nuclear weapons. China's shift of military doctrine to local border wars in the late 1980s (when Pakistan and India are believed to have crossed the nuclear weapon Rubicon) is a reflection of this factor being taken into account. International opinion (and domestic public opinion) would be strong factors pushing for early termination of such a war. This runs the risk of the war leading to a possible stalemate which could hardly serve our interests. Successful application of military power, therefore, would demand that a calibrated force is used carefully to achieve political goals and objectives. One method of applying calibrated military force would be to employ SF for defined punitive political-military goals. These forces would have to be transported by helicopters to the place of proposed action and escorted indirectly by combat aircraft. Such missions would remain an extremely high-risk and high-vulnerability even where they are of very small size and only shallow penetration into enemy territory is undertaken. Helicopters are best suited platforms for such operations. Fixed-wing aircraft do not possess the type of manoeuvrability that the helicopters are capable of. Fixed-wing aircraft would perforce have to operate at altitudes higher than those at which helicopters can fly under operational conditions and would hence be far more vulnerable with far lesser capabilities.

US SF also employs fixed-wing aircraft like the C-130 gunships. These have proved highly effective especially since they are able to deliver massive intense firepower on the target. But their utility has almost entirely been over foreign territory where no hostile air power could target these gunships. It is open to question whether such aircraft could play a useful role in the face of competent hostile air power especially when they present a large target flying at slow speed.

Third, a large quantum of our military commitments is in the high Himalayas where the army has been deployed for decades. Most of these borders are disputed with little prospect of resolution of the disputes. A major aspect of our war-fighting capability, hence, must cater for operations in high mountainous areas. Helicopters are no doubt even more vulnerable to hostile ground fire in the mountains since the rotor noise gives more than ample advance warning of helicopter approach due to noise resonance in the valleys. But compared to fixed-wing aircraft, which still need landing grounds, which are not easily available and remain, tied to available geographical rather then operational locations, helicopters provide special attributes that make them invaluable in the Himalayas. We need to look closely at the lessons of Kargil War where we do not seem to have been able to utilise army aviation for elementary reconnaissance and surveillance contributing in no small measure to the strategic and tactical surprise achieved by Pakistan Army.[1]

Overall it can be concluded that fixed-wing aircraft, as normally classified and understood, would remain an important air power component of a nation in peace and war. After all, all our combat aircraft are fixed-wing aircraft and so are the transport aircraft. By virtue of their characteristics it is neither feasible nor desirable doctrinally to make them integral to army aviation organisation. A clear example is that of the UK which designed a combat aircraft specifically for close support of the land forces, which could take off and land like a helicopter-the Harrier, but kept it as part of the RAF (rather than the army). The American version of the Harrier, the AV-8 is part of the US Marine Corps (which has its own air force and a role far beyond continental United States), but is not an integral part of the US Army.

Seen against this backdrop, the suggested vision for the Indian AAC as outlined in the concept paper in that "Army aviation must provide combat, combat support and combat service support capabilities, across the full spectrum of operations, to all field commanders,......" (emphasis added) would appear to be overly unrealistic and subject to numerous misleading interpretations and misunderstandings.[2] There is no dispute that AAC needs to be modernised, as much as all the three services themselves need to be modernised. The chances of successfully achieving such modernisation would depend on rational and objective understanding of our future needs based on sound doctrinal precepts and matching them with the likely technological and financial resources.

More specifically, the operational roles as outlined in the concept paper would have to rely heavily on fixed-wing aircraft normally part of air force.[3] Any suggestion that this is part of the role of an AAC (leave alone of land forces) is bound to generate avoidable misunderstanding detrimental to maximising joint operations, besides being in contradiction to Indian Army's latest doctrine (unless the term "air power" in the doctrine implies army aviation only!).[4] Any loose formulations affecting air power would, at the minimum, reduce mutual confidence and trust between the air force and the army, and at its maximum would make the air force as an integral component of the AAC of Indian Army.

At the same time we need to note that advances in aviation technology have made it possible for small-sized UAVs to undertake an increasing range of roles and types of missions, required in a modern battlefield.[5] While Israel had started developing remotely piloted vehicles in the 1960s and used them to great effect in 1982 Beka'a Valley operations, these have really started to play a crucial role on modern battlefield as the recent wars in Afghanistan and Iraq demonstrate. UAV systems are still quite expensive and their efficacy is largely dependent on the sensor technologies that go to make the payload. But it is quite obvious this is one of the key thrust areas for our army aviation to focus on in the coming years and decades. One hopes that the process would not get mired down in inter-service turf battles since all three services would require UAV systems tailored to their specific needs and missions, which in certain circumstances should be seen as complementary. This aspect needs greater attention, study and integration into our thinking about future military capabilities. ■

Notes:

1 *From Surprise to Reckoning,* The Kargil Review Committee Report, (New Delhi: Sage Publications, 1999), p. 88.

2 Vijay Oberoi, "Optimisation of Indian Army Aviation: An Approach," Concept Paper for the seminar on "Indian Army Aviation: 2025" organised by Centre for Land Warfare Studies, New Delhi, March 16, 2005.

3 Ibid., pp. 9-10.

4 *Indian Army Doctrine,* issued by Headquarters Army Training Command, Shimla, October 2004, p. 71.

5 For an early study see Jasjit Singh, *Air Power in Modern Warfare,* (New Delhi: Lancer International, 1985), pp. 195-209.

Indian Army Aviation Corps: Structures for Future Security Challenges and the Key Focus Areas

— **Vice Admiral Vinod Pasricha (Retired)**

"Aviation is a good sport, but for the Army it is useless."

-General Foch, French Army, 1914

"Experience has shown that a real combat in the air, such as journalists and romancers have described, should be considered a myth. The duty of the Aviator is to see, not to fight."

-German General Staff, 1915

(And yet in the last ten months of World War I, the British aircraft industry alone produced 27,000 aircraft.)

Introduction

The emergence of the third dimension drastically changed the conventional concept of warfare in just four years. And now just a century after the Wright Brothers' historic flight, the aviation today has an overarching role in all forms of warfare. Also, the speed with which technology is currently galloping, the next two decades will easily exceed the rate of change that was achieved in the entire 20th century.

The Approach Paper prepared by the Centre of Land Warfare Studies addresses issues vital for the aviation arm of the Indian Army, which could not have been better articulated. It gives examples of the structures adopted by other nations, some of whom have an aviation corps older than even IAF. These organisations have survived through World War II and many subsequent wars and battles. In contrast, the AAC is a very nascent organisation. In fact, if we follow the plan envisaged in the Accretion Plan-2017, our aviation corps would, at the very best, only be able to reach the strengths and capabilities currently available with the armies of the developed world. By that time, these countries would have graduated exponentially to far greater operational capabilities. It is, therefore, only appropriate for us to considerably widen our horizons and set ourselves the most ambitious goals and targets with a new accretion plan.

To achieve this, we need to consider a two-pronged approach. The first prong deals specifically with consolidation; of what the AAC has today and has already initiated. In this, there are many short-term targets. These must be met; the sooner the better. In my paper, I do not intend to suggest changes to the short-term targets, as mid-course corrections to the current plan would merely be counterproductive.

However, there are a number of areas in the mid-term component of this plan, which seriously impinge on the Army's strategic goals and objectives. Some of them are elementary and it is in these that the army must really think big to enable it to deal with the security challenges in the coming decades.

Aviation Roles during Land Air Battles

Technological advances, knowledge warfare, miniaturisation and the growth of information technology (IT) have changed many a concept of modern war. As the pace at which these changes are taking place is exponential, it would remain difficult to accurately predict the speed with which future wars will be fought. However, in spite of the technological advances and appearance of better and more versatile platforms in the next two decades, the common factor will remain the roles that army aviation will be required to perform. These will not be very different from the ones enumerated below:-

- Battlefield transparency and reconnaissance.
- EW and ECM.
- Airborne command posts.
- Combat fire support.
- All-weather/ night attack capability.
- Special operations, deep penetration and infiltration.
- Tactical lift, logistics and communications.
- Cas evac and rescue missions.
- NBC components of modern warfare.

In this, the one factor that remains paramount is whether it is the change in technology that will drive future doctrine or whether we need to first formulate doctrine and ensure that technology matches up with our thought processes. Whilst the former is more likely, it is extremely important that our Army Brass strives to develop technologies that would suit our future commitments and challenges. It is strongly stressed that these necessarily have to be totally indigenous if we are to use them gainfully.

Having enumerated the tasks, one needs to see how best these can be accomplished. Before I get into the debate of which service should be responsible and accountable for these roles, it would indeed be pertinent to mention that turf battles are a part of every nation's defence forces and even within each service as to which arm/ directorate must get priority. As an example, for decades there has been a debate within the navy on whether we should acquire more ships, more submarines or more aircraft. Looking at the separate medium in which these platforms operate, it becomes obvious that all three are essential for any combat, with the submarine being ideal for underwater operations. Similarly, ships and aircraft have their tasks cut out on the surface and in the air and both have their roles clearly identified in any naval engagement. It is merely the correct combined deployment of these platforms that gives the naval commander the desired tactical advantage. Similarly, the continuing debate on whether the army or the navy needs an integral aviation component is hypothetical, as each service has to retain the capacity to include air encounters as an integral part of its personal armoury.

Services: the Role Suitability

The roles that aviation needs to perform in support of the land air battle require aircrew who are totally dedicated to such tasks, requiring many years of experience and training; be it low flying skimming the trees, using night-vision devices, collecting intelligence about the enemy formations or merely directing artillery fire. To achieve a deep understanding and be able to exploit the aircraft and systems to their optimum capabilities, these aircrew would need to be associated full-time with army manoeuvres, operational thinking and ground tactics, as also spend time in the field. If an air force pilot is to reach these exacting standards, he might as well be in an olive green uniform and spend his first twenty years with the army. To my mind, the only viable option is to transfer all helicopters operating from land, including all attack helicopters, as also reassign all tasks related to disaster management and special operations to the army.

The IAF should completely relinquish helicopter flying and would still have more than enough tasks for them with the setting up of space command, the strategic airlift command and all fighter flying and heavy lift capability with them. The aspects of co-ordination between the three services and command and control are easy to achieve, if approached in the true spirit of jointmanship.

UAVs and Drones

A new force multiplier for the Indian Defence Forces has been the acquisition of UAVs by all three services. With their current capabilities they are now able to give real-time battle surveillance inputs to the commanders. Technology has already designed UAVs with an endurance of over three and a half days, as well as miniature UAVs weighing just 17 grams. With catapult launches now being planned, one can visualise greatly enhanced roles assigned to UAVs by the army for surveillance, EW, communication and data-links. In fact, we should now change their acronym to VOF (vehicles of the future). Whilst weapon delivery remains a distinct possibility with UAVs, the option of retaining manned flights for such roles would still be preferred as split-second decision-making is essential, particularly in view of the high costs of precision guided munitions, as also of large UAVs.

With proliferation of UAVs, there are important aspects regarding their command and control and of co-ordination with the army aviation platforms also operating in the same area. The need for instant reactions in modern warfare would not permit independent slots or time-sharing. Instead, concurrent flying operations merit our attention with each service operating its own UAVs. Within the army, the only option is to have these vehicles operated by army aviation. This provides the most suitable option for command and control, operational flying, simulators and more so maintenance and logistic support. This must be implemented at the earliest.

Areas for Special Focus and Structures

With this background, I will now directly approach the question of the areas that need special focus. In this, the first and definitely the major ones are indigenisation and self-reliance. Till we start building our own world-class aircraft, systems and weapons, there is really no future for India in modern warfare. Buying them will always result in our getting lower-generation and outdated technologies, with the distinct possibility of the tap being turned off at will. Given our current capability, my suggestion to build an aircraft that matches the best in the world may sound an extremely ambitious plan, but if one goes by the experience of the navy's indigenous warships, which today compare with the best in the world, it is indeed most feasible by 2020.

Since the process of building our own is time-consuming, as an immediate measure we must ensure that all future aircraft purchased from abroad are only on the express stipulation that we would build subsequent ones in India with no strings attached. This would imply a higher price at the time of initial negotiations, but the cost benefits of this are indeed tremendous, not to mention that our own defence industries would immediately graduate to a much higher plane. We thus need to shift from the current licensed production concept to local industrialisation. This implies that we would have full rights to build, modify and sell to other countries the aircraft so manufactured. With today's economic compulsions, there is no doubt that India will find foreign firms willing to deal with us on these terms. There would definitely be additional costs on royalties, but in the long-term it is a much cheaper option. Currently, Turkey has taken this stand for 91 attack helicopters that it is in the process of purchasing; much to the chagrin of the Americans, who were aiming to be the sole competitor for a licensed production contract.

As a corollary, with USA now keen on releasing dual-purpose and cutting edge technologies to India, we must endeavour to cash in. America has certainly not suddenly become philanthropic, but has an eye on our huge defence market. Despite the fact that they will remain fickle about their long-term relationship with India, our gains lie in obtaining technologies and not equipment from them. In this manner, it would not be possible for them to turn off the tap when it no longer suits their objectives.

Standardisation of aircraft within the three services is another important requirement. Admittedly, the end product may not have the exact qualitative requirements as desired by each separate service, but the gains in overhauls, 3rd and 4th line maintenance and servicing, engines and spares inventory, economics of scale, simulators, training, documentation; etc. would more than offset the losses. As a case in point, the navy had taken a conscious decision that rather than looking for a separate advanced jet trainer, we would accept the trainer selected by the IAF. In the process, the navy has gained a lot. Similarly, the navy and the army are currently looking for ten-ton helicopters for their inventories, but have had little or no interaction on this purchase. A real pity, as there is little doubt that if services undertake combined negotiations, the overall savings would be considerable. After all, the services have managed commonality reasonably well with the ALH. Why not then in our other agreements with foreign vendors? In any case, it is the systems and weapons that would be different for the two services with the basic airframe and engine remaining common. Today, nano-technology gives us the option to really miniaturise and thus the factor of 'all-up-weight' would soon lose its relevance.

In the purchase of weapons, sensors and equipments, another stipulation must be insisted upon i.e. handing over by the original equipment manufacture of all software data and the source codes. Again an expensive option, but when one looks at the possibility that today the manufacturer can remotely render any equipment or weapon dysfunctional, the additional cost becomes insignificant. Value addition to this software by India, as and when required would be an added bonus.

Another very important factor in indigenisation is the extensive use of commercially off the shelf (COTS) items in military hardware. The ruggedness that has come about in civilian use items would be adequate for most equipment. Redundancy would still be possible by using COTS items; yet a cheaper option.

The pace of war in the future would dictate that systems, sensors and equipment are able to cope with the fast changing scenarios. Thus, computerised action information, data-linking and identification friend or foe (IFF) are essential components if the army has to react with alacrity. In fact, today's civil gadgetry such as, miniaturised cameras, global positioning system (GPS), palmtops, communications, electronic devices, etc. have all made it possible to pinpoint the location of every railway wagon and container. Extrapolating this technology for army aviation merely requires identifying expertise within India or through foreign consultants to provide a vehicle identification chip so that our helicopters become aware of the position of every tank, gun and armoured vehicle in a given battle-space. Making IFF a compulsory component of this system would further ensure that our own forces are not engaged, particularly in bad weather or at night.

Smart weapons and missiles would form yet another area where the army needs to commence the indigenisation process very early. These weapons and even precision parachutes for the SF and for supply drops may be expensive, but then a single bomb from an F-117 can accomplish today what 9,000 bombs achieved in World War II. Similarly, parachute drops at night can land with accuracies of less than five metres.

Another key focus area involves the starting of a new discipline for aircrew. With the electronics and systems packages being suggested, the work-load on a single pilot would be unmanageable. There would, therefore, be a need for a separate cadre to operate systems. Rather than carry an additional pilot, it makes better sense to train an independent person who would exercise tactical control of the aircraft. The army must create this cadre early, with a few tactical controllers being immediately trained and operating with the navy. As the army systems get crystallised, such aircrew would be invaluable during negotiations involving the selection/ analysis/ production in India of future equipment on offer or being designed by our DRDO.

Command and Control

Command and control of aviation units and their joint operability is an important consideration for army aviation. At the inter-services level, it would be ideal if the air force has the responsibility for the aerospace and strategic air commands. This would include all satellite surveillance, as also the airborne warning and control (AWAC) and ISTRS, resulting in the overall picture for AD control being available. With network-centric tapping into this data, the army formation commanders, as well as the naval commanders at sea would have the details of all airborne activity and thus would be able to plan their own sorties keeping the air defence control centre in the picture. Helicopter operations, artillery firings and low level missiles would thus become individual formation decisions covering local battle areas with co-ordination of only fighter flying and long range missiles being done by the IAF using satellites and AWACs.

Within the army, the present arrangements of command and control need to be decentralised much more with integral air being available to the brigades. The present structure is cumbersome and far too slow to cope with the speed of modern warfare. Even more than the artillery, air effort has to react instantaneously. Admittedly, we are currently woefully short of aircraft resources, but the long-term plans and doctrines must be developed to allow both attack and defensive air interaction at the brigade and lower levels, with helicopter flights comprising of one or two helicopters. This policy combined with the UAVs, guns, missiles and AD weapons will ensure a proper understanding, operational training and thereafter exploitation of the total air inventory.

This would of course result in the aviation becoming a full-fledged arm with its own director general and resultant maintenance, logistics and weapon tentacles. The present arrangements of reliance on other arms for this support is not merely time-critical but also incapable of pinning responsibility and accountability where due.

Another factor governing the growth of army aviation is the career profile of its aircrew. The very rationale of army pilots manning these helicopters is continuity and an understanding of the land battle scenarios and tactics. Were this not so, an air force pilot could easily be deputed to fly these tasks. Thus the current practice of aircrew reverting back to their parent cadre after a short stint in aviation is not in the long-term interest of army aviation. Sustained build-up of rank and experience, as well as suitable experts at brigade, division and corps headquarters are a must. Such a cadre would also permit this aircrew to continue to interact with their contemporaries during professional courses and normal army assignments. The need for a larger number of young and junior officers can be met through induction of short service officers for 7 to 10 years. This would simultaneously provide the necessary growth potential for the hardcore aviators.

Jointmanship and Division of Tasks

Finally, controversies on which service should control aviation have been raging for a long time with no end in sight. Each country practises a different and individual model for its armed forces. Resistance to changes in the existing structures is aptly summed up by Alvin Toffler when he writes:

"The military, like any huge modern bureaucracy, resists innovation-especially if the change implies the downgrading of certain units and the need to learn new skill and to transcend service rivalries."

-War and Antiwar, 1993.

Turf battles are not a new phenomenon, but what is indeed worrying is the fact that national interests are on the back-burner. Why else are the army and air force not talking to each other on how the AAC must plan ahead? Are we willing to give up the vast experience of the IAF merely because of a lurking suspicion that they will again hanker to take back all aviation?

There is enough for everyone and if the three services decide that they will together formulate the military aviation policy for themselves, the bureaucrats would indeed be stumped. Thereafter, adequate money would become available to all the services. Instead, I will quote some examples on how each service is trying to do the other one down.

In 1997, the then CAS put up a paper to the Raksha Mantri (minister of defence) and the MoD as to why the navy does not need any aircraft carriers. In his wisdom, he chose to not even endorse a copy of these views to the chief of naval staff. At that time the ministry had two separate naval proposals pending with them. These have since been approved in toto, but after a delay of nearly five years. I wonder who takes the responsibility for the resultant gap in our security tasks.

The three services have negotiated totally independently with Israel for the purchase of UAVs, with each service not quite aware of the others' contracts. Surely, tremendous savings would have accrued to India by sharing maintenance, training and logistic facilities?

The navy and the IAF negotiated for the Sea Eagle air-to-surface missile with British Aerospace independently and till very late did not think it fit to learn from each other's experiences.

For nearly ten years there have been proposals for the three services to share their flight safety expertise, at least for common aircraft like the Chetaks, Dorniers and ALH. Turf battles have prevented us from any meaningful co-operation in flight safety, maintenance and training.

A Bangalore based IT firm Macmet has written the software for flight simulators for the navy and army. Whilst one understands that writing the source codes for the first time and preparing the software would have been expensive and time-consuming but, the same is not true for the subsequent systems. However, because of lack of interaction between the two services, the firm is getting away with huge profits.

Conclusion

One hears that once the Chief of Defence Staff (CDS) concept is implemented all will be resolved. I have serious doubts; as currently individual service ambitions have converted us all into ostriches. How else can one justify the false pat on the back that we keep giving ourselves about the tri-service Andaman and Nicobar Command being an overwhelming success? Are we happy with a C-in-C who has a brigade minus a battalion, two MI-8s from the IAF and less than half a dozen small craft from the navy on his orbat?

I believe it is time that the three service chiefs got together, shed their turf coats and ensured that amongst them they decide what aviation task each service must undertake and then work as a team to ensure India's security. This would put the bureaucrats and politicians in their places and result in considerable savings. Such co-operation would then make more than enough money available for all three services. None of there are outside the realm of possibility or expensive for the value that they would generate. ■

Aviation Corps of the Indian Army: Areas of Optimisation and Revitalisation to include Structures, Aviation Platforms and Doctrinal Aspects

— Lieutenant General Vinay Shankar

Introduction

The significant, multifaceted and vital role that the third dimension plays in determining the outcome of combat is unarguable. What has been in debate and in many instances hotly disputed is as to who should own the elements that operate in the third dimension: aerial combat and aerial support and service assets, and if duplication or triplication is inescapable the extent to which this should be done.

While it is agreed that technology drives the direction in which militaries evolve, yet all militaries do not follow identical modernisation or growth paths. Military and strategic culture, tradition, ethos and more importantly threat perceptions, lessons drawn from wars fought and military ambitions also impact heavily on the direction that the armed forces of a nation take.

When we look at the size and shape of the Indian Defence Forces it would be prudent to accept two basic determinants. The first is the serious limitation on resources on account of our inherent poverty, at least for the first three decades since Independence. Even in the last two decades, the economic growth rates have not yet been such that the defence spending could witness significant increase. Consequently, availability and not requirements, as a rule, have been the basis on which allocations have been made for the defence budget.

Second is the nature of combat that we have had to engage in and the territorial threats that remain in being. The wars that we have fought have at core been territorial and thus the army has had a predominant role to play. Similarly, the insurgencies that the nation has had to contend with have essentially been an army responsibility. Thus, the army has borne the greatest burden of national integrity and security.

Our security environment is witnessing significant change. Without dwelling on the global and the regional developments we must begin to anticipate the alteration in our security scenario, if for instance the character of the Kashmir issue became more benign or that we reached an agreement with China on the border issue. Such a climatic change could release substantial resources for restructuring of our defence forces, so that more could be done to improve our strategic capability. Clearly the navy needs to grow and become more potent. For the army, size could give way to modernisation. The air force would have to redefine its missions and then determine the capabilities it seeks.

Army Aviation: Doctrinal and Conceptual Issues

Fundamentals of Air Power

In my perception, if the doctrinal and the conceptual issues are first addressed and resolved, other matters like optimisation and revitalisation will automatically get addressed. Though I must emphatically add that from what I have known of the army aviation its vitality was never in doubt and therefore I do believe it is not something that ought to concern us.

When we focus on the third dimension, clearly AD with all that it connotes is the first priority. Whether this is achieved through defensive measures or a combination of offensive and defensive capabilities are matters of strategy and tactics but the requirement of aviation support to ground forces can obviously be considered only after AD has adequately been taken care of. We would do well to take note that without a reasonable level of AD, air support application for ground forces can be very vulnerable and therefore may be rendered practically ineffective.

The next priority requirement is of air space dominance. We are familiar with the terms air superiority or a favorable air situation. This again is a prerequisite for air support operations.

Unlike the previous two principles, where broadly there is agreement, in the third and fourth role of air power views are divided at least in India. Between strategic applications of air power and the requirement of close air support to ground forces we have, yet, I believe to arrive at a consensus. Therefore, at a macro level fund allocation for these aspects of our overall defence capability has yet to follow a consistent and clear path. We urgently need to deliberate this issue and arrive at an understanding that would govern our overall modernisation and force accretion plans. The CIDS could have done this. But unfortunately it remains headless and therefore toothless. And the indications are that this is unlikely to change.

Close Air Support

Most of us tend to look at close air support to the ground forces with the theories procedures and understanding that emerged after the World War II. In any case, in our context those concepts remained relevant till almost the Eighties. It is since the Eighties that we should have started thinking in terms of redefining those concepts.

The close air support concepts that we inherited were driven by the range limitations of the surveillance, target acquisition and engagement capabilities of the land based platforms. To extend this reach to cover immediate tactical and in some cases operational requirements, aerial platforms were necessary. Fighter reconnaissance, close air support missions and the erstwhile Air OP were employed for such tasks.

Since then the march of technology has altered the scenario substantially. Artillery gun ranges have increased from the 13 km of the Sixties to now 40 kms. Rocket systems are now much more accurate and their ranges are already at the 70 km level, with potential to soon reach approximately 120 kms. With improved munitions their lethality is also much greater. Missile ranges of today need no amplification. Thus, surface based firing platforms can cover the entire tactical and operational battlefield.

Given these dramatic enhancements in lethality and range of surface based platforms close air support has now to be viewed differently. The flexibility of airborne firepower and its great psychological impact on both own troops and the adversary are important considerations. We therefore must formulate a new philosophy. The quantum of close air support requirement could diminish somewhat as we progressively increase our surface based capabilities but for the foreseeable future it cannot be expected to become entirely irrelevant. While on this subject it is important to emphasise that we would be remiss in our approach if we sought to replicate the Israeli or the US model of utilising aerial platforms for delivering firepower.

What about surveillance and target acquisition or the sensor-to-shooter linkages? Without matching capability, surface based fire capabilities are virtually un- exploitable. Surface based sensor platforms can only achieve limited ranges. To match the extended ranges and reach of surface-based firing platforms, airborne sensor and communication platforms are necessary. This is an important area of force development that we must focus on. It is reassuring to observe that in recent years this requirement has begun to receive some attention.

Elevated platforms can be based on static or mobile masts, tethered balloons, helicopters, UAVs, fixed-wing aircraft and satellites; the latter three being the more useful and flexible platforms. For effective surveillance it would be seen that the third dimension is vital. I propose to address the subject of UAVs separately. It is important that this be done for a comprehensive philosophy to emerge.

Attack Helicopters

On the subject of employment of attack helicopters, my views are somewhat more conservative than most of my peers and what is today considered accepted employment philosophy. I have a hunch that my thinking is more in line with the approach of the air force on the subject. Without going into the enormously lethal and mobile capabilities of this platform I have fears of its vulnerability, especially when operating in enemy held territory beyond the frontline or the FEBA (forward edge of the battle area) or for that matter in an environment where we do not have a favorable air situation. There is yet no evidence of employment of these platforms in an operational environment where capabilities of the adversaries are not entirely unequal. These attack helicopters have been employed in situations of complete asymmetry and then too have had to take disproportionate losses. It is my contention that while for defensive operations these platforms can be a great asset to plug breaches and redress a situation of temporary imbalance, for offensive missions we have to take into account their vulnerability to shoulder-fired SAMs, other ground fire as also enemy aircraft. I am aware that this position will be hotly debated and this is how it should be, but 1 cannot resist conveying my apprehensions.

The capability accretion of attack helicopters must be done after due deliberation. Maybe a detailed study of Chechnya, Sri Lanka, Kosovo, Kargil and Iraq is mandated before we arrive at conclusions. Even though in all these instances there was no comparison in the capabilities of the adversaries. In our case the equation is unlikely to be so terribly unequal. And then there is the problem of limited employability in the Eastern theatre.

Troop Lift, Communications and Logistics

The requirements of troop lifting, communications and logistics support for the ground forces has been a contentious issue that still remains – like some of the other issues – unresolved. The operational imperative of such capability should not be questioned. The extent of the capability and the ownership issue however could be debated. The real issue is the time sensitiveness of the requirement and the responsiveness of available assets. The army from its perspective and for a variety of very legitimate reasons would obviously want to own all such assets that are currently available as also dictate the direction of capability enhancement for the future. The air force for historical reasons, economy of effort, avoidance of duplication, and apprehensions of loss of turf would resist all such moves.

Since the formation of army aviation, some water has already flown under the bridge. We must first accept that it would be unwise to try and reverse this process. The issue really is where do we go from here? Looking at the problem incrementally perhaps may be the appropriate way forward. Some plans have already been drawn up. These could be reviewed in the light of these deliberations and other such re-examination that may be undertaken. It has inevitably to be a dynamic process.

UAVs

UAVs are extremely versatile aerial platforms. While the army was first off the block in visualising and understanding its potential and has since been pursuing the acquisition of this capability, our overall procurement procedures are such that the progress has been tardy. The air force and the navy have also procured these platforms and together all the three services are currently examining the induction of a wide range of new UAVs.

I am not too sure about the other two services but I do have reason to believe that in the army a segmented view is being taken on its requirements of aerial platforms. We need to correct this. UAVs can perform most of the surveillance and target acquisition and communication (not communication sorties by commanders) functions that helicopters can undertake. UAVs can also be employed for observe and attack missions. Therefore, when we project our requirements for these capabilities a holistic view would be necessary. Such an appraisal may lead us to different priorities and a different mix of capabilities.

Ownership and Economy of Effort

Much has been said on the question of economy of effort, avoidance of duplication, optimisation of capability on the one hand and on the other the need for integration of combat and combat support elements, the imperative of unity of command and the importance of assimilation of all components into a cohesive combat organisation. To what extent these requirements are mutually exclusive is the real issue.

The positions of the army and the air force on these issues have generally been irreconcilable. Each has its own perspective. And while for years there has been across the board emphasis on the importance of bridging the divide, nothing substantive has yet been done. The best that we have done in the past is to brush issues under the carpet in order to remain on talking terms with each other. I do not quite know the methodology that can be adopted to generate a reasonable convergence of positions. I did believe that the CDS would solve most inter service issues but now that is unlikely. Let us hope that this forum can throw up some answers.

Optimisation of Army Aviation

On the subject of optimisation of army aviation, I have a few comments to offer. The first is on the legacy that the army aviation has inherited – the legacy of the erstwhile Air OP. That inheritance has had a great influence on how the army aviation has evolved. Consequently, the role of army aviation at core has remained surveillance, target acquisition and the direction of fire. The larger role that the army aviation must play has not been fully understood or assimilated by officers other than army aviators. This then is the immediate requirement that is to educate a much wider spectrum of officers at all levels on the nuances of army aviation and its employment. Optimisation can only happen when this begins.

Such exposure and education may lead to greater emphasis on army aviation in terms of its capabilities and employment concepts. It may also lead to employment philosophies that aim at greater exploitation of existing capabilities.

Conclusion

In my paper, I have not addressed specifics. Neither have I dwelt on a whole range of issues that impact on the kind of decisions we need to take on the future of army aviation. I have only dwelt on some considerations that I felt merited attention. I would tread with caution on the offensive employment of army aviation especially attack helicopters. At the same time, I would concentrate on the requirement of surveillance and helicopter lift capabilities in the mountains. Simultaneously, I would seek to view UAVs as complementary systems when addressing the overall requirement of army aviation assets. ■

Integration of Attack Helicopters with Joint Operations on Land

— **Brigadier Gurmeet Kanwal**

Joint Air land Battle

The emergence of Bangladesh as the new hub of international Islamic terrorism, the political uncertainty in Nepal and the spread of Maoist militancy across several Indian states, have added new challenges to the traditional national security threats faced by India. Given India's unstable external security environment and inimical neighbours, who lose no opportunity to exploit internal instabilities, future conventional war on land, though improbable, cannot be ruled out. In the Indian context, such a war is likely to be a point on a continuum that encompasses the present conflict along the LoC and the actual ground position line (AGPL) with Pakistan, combined with Pakistan's ongoing proxy war, and a possible "border war" along the line of actual control (LAC) with China that might spin out of the unresolved territorial and boundary dispute.

Due to the nuclear shadow hanging over the Indian subcontinent, future wars will, in all probability, be limited wars. These will be limited in political and military objectives and in terms of time and space and the application of force levels. It would be necessary to find ways and means to generate maximum firepower asymmetry in the land battle in order to impose India's will on the adversary. Consequently, it will be possible to conduct a successful land campaign only with overwhelming and sustained support from the IAF by way of closely integrated air-to-ground strikes in the contact, intermediate and the deep battles. The recent wars in Afghanistan and Iraq have conclusively proved that only a skilfully integrated and coordinated joint air land campaign can possibly achieve desired military aims in a limited war. This would be even truer in the case of OOA military interventions that must necessarily be surgically executed if they are to succeed.

Also, by now it is well recognised that EW and 'information operations' in the land battle cannot be conducted successfully without a substantial contribution from aerial strikes and EW assets. Operation Desert Storm, also known as the first information warfare (IW), highlighted the importance of information operations during limited wars. "The targets of the opening shots in Desert Storm were two Iraqi radars located just inside Iraq's border with Saudi Arabia. Hit from army helicopters firing Hellfire missiles, these stations went silent. Moments later, a stealthy F-117 launched a 2,000 pound laser-guided bomb on an interceptor control station. Those two attacks opened a door in an electronic wall through which 668 aircrafts were to streak into Iraq."[1] In future wars, a few grammes of silicon in a computer may have greater effect than a ton of depleted uranium. Under such circumstances 'jointness' in the conduct of operations will be an essential prerequisite. Only the synergised impact of individual service capabilities will ensure a positive outcome.

However, it must be clearly recognised that while future wars on the Indian subcontinent are likely to be fought as limited wars, larger conflicts cannot be ruled out. Planning and preparation for conventional war and future force structures must take this reality into account. The nation must remain prepared to come to grips with and eliminate threats across the entire spectrum of conflict. In this context, the US army's operational concept, which caters for the entire spectrum of conflict, is relevant: [2]

- The army's goal is battle-space dominance: control of the nature, scope and tempo of an operation.
- Its constant aim is to seize the initiative, maintain momentum and exploit success.
- It seeks to defeat an enemy by destroying the coherence of his operations.
- The army will operate at a tempo and intensity that enemy forces cannot match.
- The aim is to force the enemy into a turbulent, steadily deteriorating situation with which he cannot cope.

Need to Mass Firepower not Forces

It is well recognised that the concept of attacking the enemy's centre of gravity is key to all operational design. During both defensive and offensive operations in limited war, especially when deep strikes cannot be executed without the risk of escalation to nuclear war, careful consideration is necessary to determine what will constitute military objectives that have a bearing on the adversary's centre of gravity. In a complex organisation like a divisional or corps level field formation, some important components are more vital than others to the smooth and efficient operation of the whole. "If these can be damaged or destroyed, their loss unbalances the entire structure, producing a cascading deterioration in cohesion and effectiveness which may result in complete failure, and which will invariably leave the force vulnerable to further damage."[3]

The correct identification of the enemy's centre of gravity and the planning and successful execution of actions to expose it, to attack and destroy it, are the essence of operational art. Due to the ongoing revolution in military affairs (RMA), the mass of enemy forces is no longer the most vulnerable and operationally important asset of the enemy. At least in the plains, the centre of gravity of field formations is increasingly shifting towards their reconnaissance, surveillance and target acquisition (RSTA), C3I systems and long-range fire delivery means, particularly rocket launchers and SSMs. Logistics bases and lines of communications are also important enemy assets, especially in the mountains. It is these vulnerabilities that are increasingly gaining prominence as prime targets for early destruction. The successful destruction of the enemy's command centres, RSTA and firepower assets and the disruption of his intelligence communications systems will render him incapable of fighting effectively and will, hence, lead to eventual victory. Most of these "prime" targets can be successfully destroyed only by effective air-to-ground strikes launched by fighter ground attack (FGA) aircraft and attack helicopters.

When operations are conducted with a nuclear backdrop, it is axiomatic that field formations must deploy dispersed and fight concentrated. However, with the advent of revolutionary precision guided munitions (PGMs) and the artillery's ability to rapidly deliver massive fire assaults over a large number of targets with a potent mix of tube and rocket ammunition, the concentration of force, even for a short duration of time, is likely to lead to unacceptable damage and casualties. Clearly, in future the aim should be to mass firepower, not forces, to achieve military objectives and use PGMs to destroy hard targets such as tanks and bunkers, with surgical precision. PGMs also help to reduce collateral damage and casualties to civilians trapped in the battle zone.

The Tofflers, Alvin and Heidi, have emphasised the progressively greater utility of PGMs and, consequently, their importance in the de-massification of forces on the modern battlefield. Their analysis is worth repeating:[4]

> "To appreciate just how astonishing these capabilities are, it helps to glance briefly backward. In 1881, for example, a British fleet fired 3,000 shells at Egyptian forts near Alexandria. Only ten ever hit their targets.
>
> As recently as the Vietnam War American pilots flew 800 sorties and lost ten planes

in an unsuccessful attempt to knock out the Than Hoa Bridge. Later four F-4s armed with some of the earliest smart bombs did the job in a single pass.

In Vietnam, an American M-60 tank crew had to find cover, stop the tank, and aim before it could fire. At 2,000 yards, at night, the chances of hitting a target were, according to tank expert Ralph Hallenbeck, 'pretty nil'. Today the crew of an M-1 tank can fire without stopping. Night-vision aids, lasers, and computers that automatically correct for heat, wind, and other conditions assure that they will score a hit nine out of ten times.

Today one F-117, flying a single sortie and dropping one bomb, can accomplish what it took B-17 bombers flying 4,000 sorties and dropping 9,000 bombs to do during World War II, or 95 sorties and 190 bombs during Vietnam."

In future, large components of infantry and mechanised forces will be employed to act primarily as deterrent forces and will be ordered to seize and hold ground only after the massive employment of all available fire delivery means, including artillery and air power, has completely pulverised the objective and rendered it incapable of any further resistance. It will become an inescapable necessity for friendly forces to achieve such fire supremacy in the battlefield that the enemy becomes incapable of utilising his own firepower means to cause serious damage to friendly forces. In limited war, which is likely to be governed by various time and space and application of force levels limitations, it will be even more necessary to rely on the destructive potential of massed firepower. In short, major investments need to be made to upgrade future firepower capabilities by several orders of magnitude.

The battle-space of the future will be characterised by high intensity conventional operations, particularly in the plains. Sustained and accurate firepower will be a key requirement in the land battle, with greater emphasis on precision and range to maximise destruction in depth and minimise civilian casualties and collateral damage. Fast moving mechanised forces will present fleeting, well-dispersed targets. In defensive as well as offensive operations, targets will enjoy greater protection than was the ease in wars in the 20th century. The higher tempo of battle will place heavy demands on firepower as the option of choice to cause prohibitive damage to the enemy's military machine. The experience of Coalition forces during the Gulf Wars is a case in point. Robert H. Scales Jr. has written:

"There is no doubt that the American employment of firepower in the Gulf War was a success. Practical application of the precision revolution on the battlefield allowed American air and ground firepower to level Saddam's mountain of fast-class war

material in a well-conceived campaign of attrition by firepower. Victory came quickly and with few US casualties." [5]

FGA Strikes and Attack Helicopters in Joint Operations

Air Land Battle

The concept of air land battle is too well known to bear repetition. Its roots lay in the weakness of NATO's ground forces deployed in a linear manner against the Warsaw Pact's overwhelming conventional superiority and "a perceived opportunity offered by emerging technology" to overcome the shortcomings.[6] The simultaneous destruction of forces comprising the Warsaw Pact ground offensive was visualised over an extended battlefield. General Don A. Starry has written: [7]

> "The expression 'extended battlefield' was used to denote a threefold expansion of the defence. First, in depth, 'with engagement of enemy units not yet in contact to disrupt the enemy time table, complicate command and control and frustrate his plans, thus weakening his grasp on the initiative.' Second, 'the battle is extended forward in time to the point that current actions such as attack on follow-on echelons, logistical preparation and manoeuvre plans are interrelated to maximise the likelihood of winning the close battle as time goes on.' Third, the 'range of assets figuring in the battle is extended towards more emphasis on higher level army and sister service acquisition means and attack resources'."

Subsequently, NATO adopted the doctrine of follow on forces attack (FOFA), which, according to General Bernard Rogers, differed in some aspects from air land battle, "Although both incorporate some ideas which are similar, air land battle is designed to have world-wide application and carries some features that do not apply to the deterrent and offensive missions assigned to Allied Command Europe."[8] The new concepts were primarily aimed at exploiting emerging technologies to go beyond traditional interdiction tasks. By harnessing the increased range and lethality and precision-strike capability of modem air-to-surface and ground-based weapons platforms, it became possible to fight the contact, the intermediate and the depth battles almost simultaneously. More responsive C3I systems and state-of-the-art RSTA technologies enabled commanders to plan well-integrated joint operations. It became possible to achieve the paralysis inherent in Liddle Hart's indirect approach by direct means.

However, it was soon realised that concepts such as air land battle and FOFA required extremely heavy capital investments and were difficult to translate quickly into new force structures. "In 1984, General Rogers had estimated that FOFA could have been implemented with a one per cent increase in the collective budget for alliance members over 10 years. By 1990 that figure had not been raised."[9] Not all analysts readily accepted the new concepts. Steven Canby wrote: "Throughout the ages, the introduction of a qualitatively new weapon has been heralded by the prognosis that war will never again be the same. To date, these predictions have always proved false. There is no reason to believe that tactics will adjust to precision weaponry."[10]

It does not need to be emphasised that "air power will be a crucial factor... on most battlefields... There will be a premium on stand-off precision missiles which can be launched at (ground) targets from long range."[11] The concept of air land battle would become more relevant on the Indian subcontinent as RMA technologies gradually come to the forefront. Synchronised, simultaneous ground and air strikes would be needed to achieve the greatest impact. The Tofflers have argued: "Deep strikes by the air force would be needed to knock out the adversary's command centres, logistics lines, communications links and air defences. This, in turn, would require the closest integration of air and ground forces."[12] It is a well-worn military maxim that integrated and synergised strategic, operational level and tactical strikes against ground targets by ground and air forces produce a cumulative effect on the enemy.

The US Army believes that "the success of both offensive and defensive operations can depend greatly on massing air power at decisive points... Close air support enhances land force operations by providing the capability to deliver a wide range of weapons and massed firepower at decisive points."[13] Because of the high density of AD weapons in the tactical battle area (TBA), air forces all over the world are advocating that battlefield air interdiction (BAI) would provide greater payoffs than close air support missions. Jasjit Singh has written: "In the tactical area at least, the defences appear to have gained the upper hand, leading many serious experts to advocate reliance on means other than tactical air power."[14] Though not openly acknowledged, this aspect is likely to have been a key factor in the graduation to FOFA by NATO in the mid-1980s. During the Kargil conflict, some IAF aircraft dropped their bombs from distances greater than 15 km after two aircraft had been hit by SAMs. In almost all modem armies it is becoming increasingly common for planners in the corps TAC (tactical air centre) to suggest that air force assets should be exclusively utilised for BAI, as the payoffs would be much greater and the risks much lesser. One lesson that has emerged quite clearly from the recent conflicts in the Balkans, Afghanistan, and Chechnya and now in Iraq is that air power alone cannot win a modern war.

Employed in a synergistic manner in conjunction with ground forces, air power is a substantive force multiplier that can pave the way for victory. Interdiction of targets in depth and the provision of close air support to the ground forces, that is the suppression or destruction of enemy forces in contact with the army troops being supported, is now part and parcel of the tactics, techniques and procedures of conventional combat on land. Land force operations are enhanced by the capability of FGA aircraft and attack helicopters to quickly deliver a wide range of weapons and massed firepower at decisive points. In Gulf War II, the US armed forces raised close air support to the level of a fine art. Air-to-ground strikes were whistled in more frequently than in any other war and were delivered with alacrity in an unbelievable response time of 15 to 20 minutes, earning for the flyboys the sobriquet "airborne artillery".

Close Air Support

The importance of close air support in modem wars must not be underrated. It is well known that just a few missions of FGA aircraft and attack helicopters can deliver more ordnance by way of dumb 1,000-pound bombs in a few minutes on an objective for attack than a medium artillery regiment can deliver in 20 to 30 minutes. What is not so well known is that these 1,000 shells would need more than 20 vehicles and 50 to 60 soldiers to transport from ammunition depots in rear areas to the gun positions and five to six hours to prepare, everything being done manually. In critical situations, particularly in fast flowing mechanised operations, accurate air strikes can save the day. The Battle of Longewala during the 1971 War with Pakistan is a case in point. Also, it is a truism that visibly accurate air strikes against the enemy in contact provide a psychological boost to the morale of ground troops. Nothing heartens beleaguered infantrymen more than to see the enemy getting a hammering from one's own air force and artillery. In fact, the US Field Manual makes the point that 'the airspace of a theatre is as important a dimension of ground operations as the terrain itself"[15] The problem of enemy AD weapons can be overcome by evolving a coordinated suppression of enemy air defence (SEAD) plan employing artillery, attack helicopters and air and ground based EW platforms.

Indian Context

Air-to-Ground Strikes in Mountains

The mountainous terrain on India's northern borders presents peculiar professional challenges for the pilots of FGA aircraft. Defensive posts held by enemy troops are normally located on the dominating heights, while artillery gun positions, battalion and brigade headquarters; communications centres, logistics installations, loading points, vehicle parks, tactically important bridges and the barracks and stores housing uncommitted reserve troops and their arms, ammunition, rations and supplies are located in the valleys. The enemy posts on the LoC are usually of platoon strength (30 soldiers). The platoon is deployed over an area of 50 by 40 metres in three to four steel and concrete bunkers with a few emplacements for weapons such as 2-inch mortars and shoulder-fired rocket launchers. The bunkers could be double-storey with the upper one designed as a fighting bunker and the lower one, usually underground, for living.

The widely separated posts are "sited for all round defence" on high mountaintops or along the sharp spines of narrow ridgelines or spurs and present small targets that cannot be easily acquired visually and are difficult to attack from the air as even a near miss by a dumb bomb can make it explode uselessly, up to a kilometre away. The targets in the valleys lie along the banks of twisting and turning rivers and nullahs. The valleys are deep and tucked between sharply rising hillsides and are not easily approached by low-flying, fast moving FGA aircraft. It is an enormous challenge for a young fighter pilot to dive into a narrow valley, navigate his aircraft to the weapon release point and deliver his payload accurately on the target. If these targets are to be successfully engaged, double or even triple the required number of missions must to be planned to achieve the desired result.

Careful cost-benefit analysis would often reveal that with the aerial delivery platforms and air-to-ground weapons available at present, the effort necessary is simply not commensurate with the results that might be achieved. To some extent this challenge could be overcome by employing attack helicopters. However, as the Afghan resistance proved against the Soviets and as was witnessed during the Kargil conflict, these lumbering fighting machines are extremely vulnerable to shoulder-fired SAMs. Since India is more likely to fight future border wars in the mountains than in the plains, as in the past, this shortcoming needs to be addressed early.

The LIC

The remaining roots of Pakistan's continuing proxy war in Kashmir are now mainly located in Pakistan Occupied Kashmir (POK) and across India's western border in Pakistan's heartland itself. A large number of terrorist training camps, assembly areas and launch pads are located across the LoC in POK. One or more major incidents of Pakistan-sponsored terrorism may compel India to launch air strikes across the LoC at some of these camps. Air Marshal Patney is of the view: "If we are really serious about ending cross-border terrorism, the air force needs to cross the Line (LoC) more often... The army's organic weapons have limited range and yield limited options. The use of aircraft will permit better selection of targets at considerable distances with more effective weapons. Moreover, the use of air power does not involve any desire to gain territory and, therefore, is not escalatory in that sense. In any case, it has now become necessary." 16 Whether or not the use of air power across the LoC is escalatory is a debatable issue. What is beyond doubt is that should the pursuit of such a course of action become necessary in the unending fight against Pakistan-sponsored trans-border terrorism, the IAF and the army should be well prepared for the joint orchestration of this option.

Under certain circumstances, to intercept infiltrating or exfiltrating bands of terrorists, India may even exercise its right of hot pursuit, as prevalent in and sanctified by international law. Hot pursuit operations would need to be supported by closely coordinated FGA and attack helicopter strikes and may also require transport helicopters to move reserve troops quickly to their release or drop-off points, close to or even across the LoC and to retrieve them after the operation. Such an operation would require fighter and attack helicopter escort for the utility helicopters, during both infiltration and exfiltration phases. Since trans-LoC operations would invariably be undertaken at night or in hours of poor visibility, it would be mandatory for the participating IAF units to be capable of night- flying and accurate navigation to the release or drop-off points and to be trained for suchs specialised operations.

Also, the RSTA capabilities required for successful air-to-ground strikes must not be lost sight of. In an interview on the eve of Air Force Day recently, Air Chief Marshal S. Krishnaswamy highlighted several emerging technologies that he felt were critical to enable the IAF to maintain superiority in the South Asian region. Among these, he was of the view, were "sensors, specifically those that can be employed for target acquisition by night and bad weather... (and) stand-off short/ long-range precision guided weapons that could be launched from multiple types of carriers like helicopters and combat aircraft."[17]

Superior precision firepower, delivered from ground-based and aerial platforms, can give ground forces a decisive edge in limited wars. Long-range lethal munitions and precision targeting promise to provide an immense edge to well-equipped ground forces. According to Robert H. Scales Jr., "the lesson from the Gulf War is clear: in a high intensity war, firepower must break the enemy's will to resist before close combat begins. Firepower must so weaken the enemy that close-in killing by infantry and armoured forces becomes a coup de grace rather than a bloody battle of attrition."[18] The Indian army's recent experience in Kargil has also provided the same lesson. Maximum Indian casualties occurred during initial assaults on the icy mountaintops occupied by regular Pakistani soldiers, before the artillery had built up to the level of being able to concentrate 100 guns on each target in turn. Sustained, accurate and high volume concentrated artillery firepower eventually won the battle for India by completely decimating enemy *sangars* (field fortifications built from loose rocks) and enabling the infantry to assault virtually unopposed. Tiger Hill and many other objectives were finally re-captured without a single casualty. Air strikes by the IAF were also instrumental in weakening the enemy's resolve. The battle winning utility of ground and air firepower in limited wars was established beyond doubt.

Supporting SF Operations

During limited war, due to restrictions on the level of application of force and other limitations, operations by SF assume even greater importance than in full-scale operations in aiding the commander's design of battle. SF units can conduct either unconventional warfare or act unilaterally in the enemy's rear areas in support of ground operations. Unconventional warfare operations can concentrate on strategic and operational level goals and may aim to achieve either immediate or long-range effects on the conflict. Such operations could include interdicting enemy lines of communications and locating, identifying and destroying important military targets. SF units would also be employed to collect strategic intelligence and conduct psychological operations when necessary. The greatest value of SF units to commanders at all levels is to add depth to the ground operations, forcing the enemy to deploy a large number of combat forces to protect his rear areas. The most desirable method of insertion of SF units behind enemy lines is by helicopters, supported by attack helicopters and FGA strikes.

Air Assault Capability

The need for surprise is even greater in limited war than in full-scale conventional conflict because of the many restrictions imposed on the conduct of operations. In what is generally regarded as his most important contribution to military thinking, Boney Fuller has made an important distinction between 'moral' and 'material' surprise. Moral surprise, he avers, means that the enemy is unaware that you are coming and material surprise means that the enemy knows that you are coming but can do nothing to stop you.[19] In Fuller's opinion, only moral surprise can achieve an immediate decision. The component of modern forces that is most suitable for achieving tactical and sometimes even operational level surprise is an air assault formation that is self-contained in combat helicopter lift capability. An air assault brigade is capable of achieving both moral and material surprise through its speedy deployment from an unexpected direction. One of the reasons for this is that helicopters can use ground tactically without depending on it for mobility.[20] An air assault formation can move dispersed and fight concentrated. Soft targets such as command and communications centres, forward airfields, important bridges, logistics installations and SSM hides could form primary objectives for wreaking havoc in the enemy's rear at operational depth.

The selection of objectives would also be dependent on the ability of ground assault forces to ensure a timely link-up. Also, with its growing regional responsibilities and increasing calls for joint international action, as also to defend its island territories and its exclusive economic zone, India needs to develop a potent air assault capability. However, an air assault brigade would cost the equivalent of a light armoured division to raise and maintain. Force multipliers are sometimes budget multipliers too! All of these critical capabilities require a fleet of combat helicopters that are specially designed for the purpose. These must be acquired in sufficient numbers, progressively increasing the total capability to at least one air assault brigade over a decade. This is another military endeavour in which attack helicopters play a significant role during all stages of the operations.

Joint Air Attack Teams

The FGA aircraft are finding it increasingly difficult to penetrate the dense AD umbrellas of manoeuvre forces to launch effective air strikes. Secondly, the EW measures adopted by the enemy successfully degrade the capability of FGA missions to deliver their lethal payload within acceptable limits of accuracy. Low survivability and reduced effectiveness of FGA missions are bound to cause considerable anxiety. This is applicable with a variation of only one order of magnitude to strikes by attack helicopters. Hence, the SEAD is rapidly becoming a high priority task whenever FGA or attack helicopters missions are planned while operating in a high density AD environment.

During a LO-LO-LO attack mode, flying just above the tree tops at supersonic speeds, an FGA mission pilot's time-over-target is not adequate to allow acquisition and engagement to the desired accuracy. He would need help by way of guidance from a heliborne FAC and for unmistakable mission effectiveness. Ideally, FGA missions should be integrated with army aviation assets and indirect fire support from the artillery. Such a concerted employment of air support resources would be a potent combat force multiplier and would result in the optimum utilisation of valuable and scarce assets.

One method of achieving the necessary integration and close cooperation is by forming JAAT -an idea whose time has come. The JAAT provides the ground formation commander with a highly mobile lethal force, capable of engaging enemy forces beyond the range of ground-based direct firing weapons, well before the enemy forces establish contact with own troops or mechanised forces. The JAAT can delay, disrupt or destroy enemy manoeuvre elements in any tactical situation, help contain enemy penetrations and provide commanders with useful information about enemy dispositions, locations and activities. The flexibility of JAAT can be employed to maintain continuous pressure on mobile enemy forces beyond the range of ground-based weapons, particularly in situations of dire emergency, such as when a helicopter-borne force is counter-attacked by enemy armour before link-up can take place.

Skilful execution is necessary to orchestrate the MAT concept successfully. Scout helicopters reconnoitre the target area for firing positions for attack helicopters, also called battle positions, suitable directions of approach, locations of enemy AD weapons launchers and command and control vehicles, choke-points and bottlenecks through which enemy forces may pass and potential engagement areas. On locating and identifying the enemy elements to be attacked, they ensure that visual contact is maintained throughout the operation. Subsequently, during the attack, the scouts provide visual security for attack helicopters. The FGA aircraft usually enter the target area in a two-aircraft flight as the basic attack configuration. Terrain and weather influence the number of flights which can operate in a target area at one time. FGA aircraft commence moving for the strike from the control point using low-altitude tactical navigation to draw maximum advantage from contour masking. The FAC or airborne controller provides updated information as necessary and gives the final attack clearance.

Limitations and Recommendations

It has been argued before that "Like artillery fire, there is now an inescapable need for immediate air support to also be 'on call' so that it can be delivered in real-time. Even for pre-planned air support, it is unrealistic to ask the corps staff to plan 24 hours in advance. Pre-planned air support should be available to a commander in the field at two hours notice - the usual response time for reacting to emerging situations."[21] If attack helicopters were considered to be the 'fourth squadron' of a combat group, the time has come for dedicated close air support assets to act as the 'fifth squadron', particularly during offensive operations so that fleeting opportunities can be optimally exploited. However, the degree of "jointness" necessary to successfully orchestrate FGA and attack helicopter air-to-ground strikes is lacking in the Indian context. The procedures for calling for attack helicopter strikes are still cumbersome and mired in red tape. Attack helicopter pilots are unable to recognise static targets today, particularly those under camouflage nets or those that are skilfully tucked in by exploiting terrain features and the local vegetation. Rarely do all the attack helicopter pilots of a supporting squadron attend a brigade/ combat command-level TEWT (tactical exercise without troops) or even a full-fledged field exercise when such an event should be the topmost item on their training calendar.

Attack helicopter units must be under "operational control" of the army formation that they are supporting and must form part of the planning process at every stage. The pilots must train together with the combat groups and combat commands that they will support during war. They should be able to understand each other's radio telephony procedures and methods of target indication. They must serve on each other's staff in various headquarters and must literally live and eat together, virtually on a daily basis. Live firing exercises conducted by attack helicopter units must be witnessed by officers and soldiers of the supported formations. In fact, they must be umpires on the pilots for the tactical training aspects. More attention needs to be paid to peace-time "operational-familiarisation" and "operational-reconnaissance" along the international boundary and the terrain in the areas of interest for offensive operations. Only then will the standard of coordination and understanding reach a level that will withstand the fog of war.

The number of attack helicopter units available to support ground operations is inadequate for the threats and challenges with which the army will need to cope over the next few decades. Also, while the intention here is not to go into "ownership" or equipment-related issues, clearly the MI-35 is unsuitable for future conflict on land. A much smaller helicopter capable of nap-of-the-earth flying, that packs a more potent punch and is less vulnerable to AD weapons, like the AH-64 Apache or a more modern version of the Huey Cobra, is required. Indian attack helicopters must be capable of night attack and all-weather flying. These must be able to lay-off in and operate off small helipads in forward hides where the pilots can be briefed in real-time and should need to return to FAARP for ammunition replenishment, refuelling and maintenance checks only for short durations. In other words, attack helicopters need to become a well-knit and finely integrated part of the ground battle scenario with the only difference being that they launch their lethal payload while being airborne. ■

Notes:

1. Alan D. Campen, The First Information War (New Delhi: Bookmart Publishers, in association with Armed Forces Communications & Electronics Association Press, USA, 1999), p. xiv.
2. "The Army's Operational Concept", Field Manual 100-5, Operations, 1998, (Washington, D.C.: US Army Training and Doctrine Command, Headquarters, Department of the Army, 1998).
3. "Key Concepts of Operational Design", Field Manual 100-5, Operations, 1986, (Washington, D.C.: US Army Training and Doctrine Command, Headquarters, Department of the Army, 1986), pp. 179-180.
4. Alvin and Heidi Toffler, "Third Wave War", War and Anti-War: Survival at the Dawn of the 21st Century (London: Warner Books, 1994), pp.90-92.
5. Robert H. Scales Jr., "Firepower in Future Limited War", Firepower in Limited War (Dehradun, India: The English Book Depot, 1998), pp. 287-296.
6. Tony Mason, Air Power: A Centennial Appraisal (London: Brasseys, 1994), p. 98.
7. General Don A. Starry, "Extending the Battlefield", Military Review, March 1981, p. 32, quoted by Tony Mason, n. 6.
8. General Bernard Rogers, "Greater Flexibility for NATO's Flexible Response", Strategic Review, Spring 1983, p. 12.
9. n.6, p.101.
10. Steven L. Canby, "The Conventional Defence of Europe: The Operational Limits of Emerging Technology", Working Paper 55, International Security Studies Programme, The Wilson Centre, April 1984, p.5, quoted by Tony Mason, n. 6.
11. "The Future Shape of Our Forces", The Strategic Defence Review (London: The Stationery Office, 1998), p. 22.
12. n. 4, p 64.
13. n. 2, pp. 47-49.
14. Jasjit Singh, "Offensive Air Support of Land Forces", Air Power in Modern Warfare (New Delhi: Lancer International, 1985,), pp. 162-214.
15. n. 7, p 4.
16. Several serving and retired senior IAF officers have advocated the need for trans-LoC' air strikes. See, for example, Vinod Patney, "Give Wing to Escalation Across LoC",

The Indian Express, August 27, 2002. (The author, a retired Air Marshal, was AOC-in-C, Western Air Command during the Kargil conflict.)

17. S. Krishnaswamy "Firing Line: MiGs not Technically Unsound", The Indian Express, October 6, 2002.
18. n. 5.
19. Major General J. F. C. Fuller, Foundations of the Science of War (London: Hutchinson, 1926), quoted by Brigadier (Retired) Richard E. Simpkin, Race to the Swift (London: Brasseys, 1985).
20. Brigadier (Retired) Richard E. Simpkin, Anti-tank: An Air-mechanised Response to Armoured Threats in the 90s (London: Pergamon-Brasseys, 1982).
21. Gurmeet Kanwal, "Strike Corps Offensive Operations-Imperatives for Success", Indian Defence Review, January 1988, p. 88.

Requirement of Fixed-Wing Aircraft for Indian Army Aviation

— Lieutenant General Amitava Mukherjee

Introduction

The Indian AAC is presently going through a critical period in its evolution, with an ageing organic rotary-wing fleet restricted to reconnaissance, observation and utility roles, an anachronistic dual- control over attack helicopters, and no control over medium lift helicopters (so essential for the army's air assault and logistic roles), which remain part of the air force inventory. A glaring operational void in this context, is the requirement of fixed-wing aircraft by army aviation for prosecuting effective combined arms warfare in these troubled times. While concerted efforts are ongoing to modernise the rotary-wing fleet by suitable replacement of the versatile, ubiquitous Cheetah R&O helicopter and induction of the promising ALH (Dhruva) in its armed and multi-role utility versions, enough attention has not been paid to the urgent requirement of inducting fixed-wing aircraft in a variety of roles necessary to fulfil AAC's mission as part of the combined arms team.

It is interesting to note that worldwide, army aviation evolved from fixed-wing aircraft, right from the early piston-engine biplanes and light mono- wing planes such as the legendary Russian AN-2 and the British Auster, both of which won accolades during World War II. In fact the very first Indian army aviation (then called Air OP squadrons, which were air force units under army's operational control) flying machine was the famous fixed-wing Auster Mk6 & Mk9 Air OP aircraft, which earned many laurels in all the major wars fought by independent India. In the interregnum, before the induction of the rotary-wing family of the Alouette Cheetah and Chetak, the HAL- designed Krishak, originally meant for crop spraying, complemented the vintage Auster Mk9 as a stop-gap measure. Pakistan army aviation which stole an evolutionary lead in establishing a separate operational identity long before its Indian counterpart had the US 01 Bird Dog light fixed-wing aircraft during the 1965 and 1971 Wars and still retains the fixed-wing Mushak aircraft in a variety of roles. Similarly, all major Armies such as in US, UK, Russia and China, have a variety of fixed-wing aircraft in their integral aviation branches, based on sound operational logic for various combat, combat support and logistic support functions as well as for SF. It is indeed a matter of regret that the operational requirement, induction and control of fixed-wing aircraft for army aviation, have fallen victim to the internecine turf wars between the army and the air force.

Operational Requirement of Fixed-Wing Aircraft

After the advent of rotary-wing aircraft during the World War II in the form of the auto-gyro, with its unique aerodynamic capabilities of very high manoeuvrability, vertical take off and landing and its unique hovering capability, this new flying machine was perceived as the ideal platform for all the missions of army aviation. By the 1970s, most of the major armed forces of the world had switched over from fixed-wing to rotary-wing for their major combat missions, while retaining significant numbers of fixed-wing aircraft for combat support and logistic missions in the battlefield. In India, a major policy decision was taken for a total change over of the Air OP squadrons from fixed-wing to rotary-wing and by the 1980s the process of conversion training and logistics had been completed. After over a decade of protracted and sometimes acrimonious wrangling between the army and the air force , the government decision to establish the AAC in 1987, was a half-baked compromise, particularly with regard to the control, ownership and management of the main offensive element of army aviation i.e. attack helicopters and the total lack of control over the large fleet of medium lift helicopters whose sole justification for acquisition by the air force, was the army's growing operational requirement for air assault and logistic tasks. The army's need for fixed-wing aircraft support whenever projected to the air force was generally not committed in a satisfactory manner for effective integrated planning, while the government response in this regard was at best non-committal if not indecisive. The operational necessity to augment the family of rotary-wing aircraft in the AAC flowed from certain inherent limitations of the very design of this unique flying platform. The main drawbacks were the limited range and endurance of the helicopter, its acute vulnerability to ground-based AD guns/ missiles and automatic small arms fires, complexity of logistics and maintenance, high cost per unit aircraft, and severe limitations of payload. Moreover, it was not the best platform for mounting multiple electronic or electro-optical sensors along with its associated data processing and communication systems.

Though hypothetically, in an ideal situation of integrated operational planning, the army's requirement for fixed-wing support could be provided by the air force, the ground reality as perceived by the army was that the rigid air force concept of unity of air power and its penchant for centralised control, militated against the army's essential need for reliable and responsive support in a fast moving, short duration manoeuvre warfare. Additionally, lack of sufficient autonomy at the tactical and operational levels of war, over the control and tasking of fixed-wing air assets, adversely affected the integrated application of combat power, so essential for success in battle. It would therefore be essential to examine in some detail the roles and missions of fixed-wing aircraft as an integral component of any modern AAC.

Roles and Missions of Fixed-Wing Aircraft for Army Aviation

Fixed-wing aircraft perform a variety of roles and missions to both complement and supplement rotary-wing aircraft, which are summarised below:-

- **Combat Missions.**
  - **Reconnaissance, Observation & Surveillance.** Reconnaissance operations obtain by visual observation or by other optical, electro-optical or electronic means, enemy information regarding his location, activities and potential threat. Whereas light rotary-wing aircraft provide the ideal platform for close reconnaissance, observation, and direction of artillery fire but, it is tailor-made fixed-wing aircraft capable of operating from forward advance landing grounds (ALGs), and designed to conduct in-depth reconnaissance operations from a standoff mode, which effectively extend the surveillance zone covered by ground reconnaissance platforms into the enemy's operational depth in a secure fashion. This ability to carry out reconnaissance, surveillance and target acquisition of the location of the enemy corps reserves, command/ control centres , and long-range surface-to-surface artillery, is vital for optimum positioning of own manoeuvre forces and hitting/ destroying these key enemy targets with long-range precision strike weapons. This aspect will be further examined subsequently.
  - **EW.** Though medium lift helicopters can be employed in the EW role, but due to endurance and payload limitations, fixed-wing aircraft specially fitted with communication intelligence (COMINT), electronic intelligence (ELINT) devices, backed up with integrated communication and non-communication ESM/ ECM systems and interfaced with the

command, control, communications, computers, intelligence, sensors and reconnaissance (C4ISR) system of the ground forces, are better suited to act as a powerful force multiplier in achieving information domination so essential to turn the tide of battle. Early determination of the enemy electronic orbat, along with the fixation of his major C3I emitters can enable devastating precision strikes against enemy command/ control centres and sensors, thereby paralysing his information and decision-making system.

- **Air Assault Operations.** Air assault operations are highly complex integrated operations in which air assault forces, primarily based on a combination of attack and medium/ heavy lift helicopters, employ their integral firepower, and mobility, under a cover of effective AD suppression, engage and destroy enemy forces, at critical points with a view to capture key terrain, thereby providing the decisive momentum to overall mission accomplishment. In order to sustain the momentum of such operations, it would be eminently desirable to employ fixed-wing aircraft operating from forward ALGs for troop reinforcement and essential replenishment of munitions and supplies, to augment the staying power of the air assault force. A good example of such fixed-wing aircraft was the erstwhile Canadian Caribou and the existing Lockheed Martin C-27 Spartan, which is a vastly shrunk version of the C-130 Hercules with two engines. Successful conduct of air assault operations demands a very high level of synchronisation of reliable intelligence with precision supporting fires by ground attack fighters and attack helicopters, followed by swift insertion of the air assault force duly supported by rotary and fixed-wing aircraft based reinforcements of men and material.

• Combat Support and Logistic Support Missions.

- **Command and Control Operations.** Maintaining effective command and control in the fog of war is critical to the success of any operation. Airborne command posts based on fixed-wing aircraft, equipped with communications and data processing/ display systems can enable the commander to "see" the battlefield, direct precision fires and relocate his manoeuvre forces to unhinge the enemy. The speed, flexibility and communications assets inherent in an elevated fixed-wing platform also contribute to more efficient intelligence gathering and operational decision-making, particularly for achieving optimum concentration of combat forces synchronised with precision strikes in a deconflicted (sic) manner. The fixed-wing airborne platform, with its longer loiter capability and heavier pay loads for the wide range of HF/ VHF/ UHF and allied data processing equipment, is far better suited for this role as compared to a rotary-wing platform.

- **Air Movement.** Air movement operations are conducted both during defensive/ offensive operations, to reposition critical combat elements, replenishment of munitions, equipment and supplies in support of current and/ or future operations. The most operationally responsive air movement can only be achieved by a combination of air landed or air dropped operations by rotary and fixed-wing aircraft, which are organic to army aviation.
- **Aerial Mine Warfare.** Air-delivered mines can support tactical operations by emplacing tactical minefields, reinforcing existing obstacles, closing lanes, gaps and defiles and protecting exposed flanks in a speedy fashion in mobile high-tempo operations. Medium lift helicopters and fixed-wing aircraft integral to army aviation are best suited for this role.
- **Cas Evac.** Timely evacuation of casualties from the forward battlefield to initial treatment facilities by ambulance vehicles and their subsequent movement to field hospitals in the corps zone by a combination of army aviation helicopters and fixed-wing aircraft modified to carry casualties, is a very important morale boosting factor contributing to saving lives and recycling combat manpower back into battle.

Employment of Fixed-Wing Aircraft in the Surveillance Role

As discussed above, light fixed-wing army aviation aircraft of the Dornier class, indigenously manufactured by HAL, is the ideal platform for mounting a combination of long-range oblique photography (LOROP), electro-optical sensors and synthetic aperture radars (SARs) which would provide an integrated intelligence, surveillance and reconnaissance (ISR) suite networked with the army's C4ISR system at the tactical and operational levels of war. Currently, this vital standoff airborne ground surveillance role remains an operational grey area inadequately performed by the air force.

A suitable Dornier mounted sideways looking SAR can function as an effective airborne ground surveillance system with the following major capabilities:-

- Depth of coverage 100-200 kms up to the enemy's operational depth.
- All-weather surveillance capability provided by the SAR employing the

moving target indication (MTI) mode for detection of critical moving ground targets such as enemy armour reserves manoeuvring under cover of darkness and the SAR mode for high resolution radar imagery. It may be mentioned that the latest generation of IR/ thermal imaging (TI) based electro-optical sensors mounted on the present rotary-wing or UAV based platforms do not provide reliable all-weather capability.

- On-board radar imagery data processing by suitable computerised software.
- UHF air-to-ground data links for real-time transmission of imaging intelligence IMINT data to the BSS/C4ISR node at corps level.

Requirement of Fixed-Wing Aircraft for SF Aviation

Doctrinally, SF are strategic forces which carry out vital missions in a variety of crises or conflicts below the threshold of conventional war and act as a potent force multiplier during major conflicts in conventional warfare. Some of the main core missions are during unconventional warfare: CT, direct action, short duration strikes on strategic targets, psychological and information operations. SF aviation employing a combination of rotary-wing and light fixed-wing aircraft perform a variety of tasks such as rapid aerial infiltration and penetration by special ram air parachute equipment from a standoff mode, precision attack by fixed-wing gunship in LIC/ CI operations, and special reconnaissance missions equipped with tailor-made multiple sensors.

Ideally, SF fixed-wing aviation should be integrated into a single cohesive set up for imbibing the unique training and operational culture essential for successful mission accomplishment. An alternate option would be to create specially trained and equipped rotary and fixed-wing squadrons under army aviation but operationally grouped with the SF for optimum results.

Organisational and Equipment Options

- **Organisational Options.** Considering the reality of inter-service rivalry and sensitivities concerning the subject of requirement and ownership of fixed-wing aircraft for army aviation, two options are possible. The first option is to create fixed-wing squadrons organic to the army aviation forces at corps/ theatre level. Initially, the scale should be one squadron per command with priority for the western and northern theatres. The second option is to create army aviation fixed-wing squadrons under the air force at the air command level on the same lines as the existing attack helicopter squadrons and place them under army control for training and operations. Considering the experience of the actual employment of attack helicopters in support of army operations, the existing arrangements of dual command and control have actually resulted in sub-optimal utilisation of this unique weapons' platform. Therefore from the point of view of exploiting the versatile capabilities of fixed-wing aircraft, as discussed above, in an optimal fashion, it would be most desirable to exercise the first option and create the required fixed-wing army aviation squadrons fully integrated with the army's fighting formations. Similar options are feasible for SF fixed-wing aviation, which could be structured under an integrated set up for the SF visualised in future.

- **Equipment Options.** The existing indigenous HAL manufactured Dornier fixed-wing light cargo aircraft provides the best and the quickest option as the most suitable platform for the army aviation and SF roles discussed above. Here, the naval experience of employing the Dornier as a versatile ELINT and SAR platform with on-board data processing system and data links to surface command and control systems, merits study and emulation. Besides, the short take-off and landing capabilities of the Dornier and its ability to operate from rough improvised airstrips, makes it an ideal platform for rapid troop lift and other combat support tasks in the plains and mountains, both in conventional war and CI operations in a much more time responsive manner as compared with the existing arrangements with the air force.

Future Trends

While the army has drawn up comprehensive plans for the modernisation of the rotary-wing army aviation fleet and is continuing its efforts with the MoD to rationalise the anomalous and dysfunctional command and control arrangements for attack helicopters and take over the medium lift helicopters from the IAF, there is a need to pursue new technological thrust areas which combine the virtues of the rotary-wing and fixed-wing platforms into a single integrated platform for the AAC of the future. This is the tilt-rotor, a unique aircraft designed to combine the vertical manoeuvrability and hover capability of a helicopter with long-range, endurance and greater payload of a fixed-wing aircraft. This versatility is achieved by placing propellers and their engines at the tips of the wings and enabling the propellers to pivot from the vertical to the horizontal axis while in flight. The tilt rotor aircraft can thus ascend straight up like a helicopter and then convert to cruising horizontally like a conventional turbo prop aircraft. A prototype of this hybrid aircraft has been under development in the USA for the last two decades as part of a Joint Services Advanced Vertical Lift Aircraft project and is now coming to fruition in the form of the V-22 Osprey which is currently entering service with the US Marine Corps and the US navy. The US Army Aviation has, due to resource constraints, instead opted for a future inter-theatre cargo plane to replace the C-23 Sherpa as part of its force transformation plans. In this regard, the Indian AAC needs to evaluate the cost-effectiveness of both these options in its future modernisation plans.

Conclusion

Currently, the AAC is in a state of flux, with urgent demand of resources for modernisation of its R&O fleet and obtaining MoD approval for early transfer of the attack helicopter and the medium lift helicopter fleet from the IAF to the army. In addition, in order to realise the full potential of its combat power, there is an urgent requirement to induct suitable fixed-wing aircraft to complement the rotary-wing platforms and perform key operational tasks essential for mission accomplishment. ■

New Delhi Seminar:

Excerpts from Interactive Session

Vice Admiral S.C. Chopra

Good morning ladies and gentlemen. It is indeed a pleasure to start first session this morning after an interesting talk by Vijay Oberoi. I was privy to his paper in which he had mentioned somewhere, which still sticks in my mind that General JN Choudhary who was COAS in 1963 was the first General who wanted AAC, but it took 23 years after his desire for the AAC to see the light of the day. There is a little story behind it, which I cannot resist telling you. In 1953, when I was just a sub lieutenant, there were a series of lectures being given in Delhi; one of the lecture was on naval aviation, the chairman of that particular session was Major General Choudhary and the lecture was given by a gentlemen called Captain Smallwood. He was director of the naval air staff. Captain Smallwood informed the audience that he was going to talk about the naval aviation and Indian Navy's plans to raise it. He put across very forcefully, why India must have naval aviation. Why an aircraft carrier was an essential part of a blue water navy? At the end of the lecture he could convince that large audience and media persons. It was very well reported lecture, indeed. I still have a copy of that lecture, which I picked up in Cochin in 1953.

Ladies and Gentlemen, within seven years of that talk the Indian Navy had commissioned INS Vikrant. We had trained pilots, air crews, ground crews, ship maintenance staff and all that was needed.

The second point is that when Captain Smallwood was going around and talking to every body that navy had to have an aircraft carrier, the air force always said that navy does not require it. The air force will do the job for the navy.

He went to the bureaucrats who said, "We have no such money. What are you talking about?" And within the navy, everybody told Caption Smallwood, "Why do you need aircrafts, we have got guns. They do a much better job than the aircraft." So, with all these road-blocks, in seven years. INS Vikrant was commissioned, arrived in Bombay in the eighth year. When we are talking in terms of rejuvenating the AAC, I thought I must give this little story to everybody to reflect upon.

Air Marshal Vinod Patney

We indeed had a very interesting and knowledgeable morning. But Mr Chairman, as we discussed army aviation here, ten yards away in the adjoining room in the USI, there is a talk on aerospace defence. I cannot help but think, that this represents a very wide spectrum, which the air power represents and the air power encompasses. There is another reason why I have mentioned aerospace defence. We are taking about 2025, twenty years hence. Can we go back twenty years and see what was the situation in 1985? Just to mention a few things, we did not really have cell phones, the cordless had not really come in, we were still in the incipient stage of the VCR, leave alone the DVD, and the hundred odd channels on the cable TV was a distant dream.

The Microsoft did not exist. There was no Internet. All this has taken place within the last 20 years. Soviet Union was there, Germany was divided, Kashmir was a tourists' paradise. So much has happened in these two decades.

On the military field, just take a look as to what took place. The sort of wars that have taken place since 1986 and there have been many. The first Gulf War-revolutionised warfare and brought in to currency the term RMA. Since then we have had Kosovo – the Bosnia Conflict. Kosovo, for instance, where the entire war on the part of the Allies was fought by air power; a singular exception possibly. But it is true, it has happened. Then we had Afghanistan. We also had the Second Gulf War or the Iraqi War now. We have had our Kargil and Parakram. And all these are now indicative as to which is the way forward. I think by not recognising that there is a rapid change that is taking place would be to look and fly in the face of reality.

This being the case, the theme that I have chosen for the little time that I have here is that army aviation, naval aviation and air force aviation are all part but subservient to national air power. It is the national air power capabilities and exploitation that is of concern and importance. I must mention that over here the army has been singularly good in the rapid progress that it has made in increasing its strength. Eight squadrons to 11 squadrons in about 13 years, plus the ALH. Somehow the UAVs were not mentioned and I think the UAVs are that much more important. And if you calculate all this -it is about 30-40 per cent increase. At the same time as far as the air force is concerned we have had 30-40 per cent decrease during the same period.

So when we speak about national air power, it is a matter of concern as to what is happening (to air force). Without doubt, as far as history is concerned, different countries at different times had different requirements and different operational imperatives. But there are a few points to ponder. May I suggest that within our capability, ever since I can remember, we have had most of these tasks, which were spoken of today, within the capability of the army and air force and we have tried to do these, with whatever was available. Nothing over here really came as a surprise. Without doubt, operational role and utilisation are a function of the available assets. On that basis we decide what should be the operational planning. But when it comes to the question of operational planning, as to what to do tomorrow, no one talks about doctrine, what is expected of us (services) and how do we intend to get it done. Planning for procurement is a function of what are we going to get from where with the available money. The prioritisation must be set and I again repeat the theme that one must look at as national air power capability, and once we get that clear it will be that much simpler.

I ask a simple question, let us do an audit, we have had army aviation for 20 years, and how has it changed our capabilities? We will not talk about the ease of administration, the ease with which the utilisaiton of these machines for the army has taken place. How has it changed our operational capabilities? Did army aviation in its fledgling state that we have at present support us in Kargil? Or for that matter support us during Parakram? Did it support us in the ongoing insurgency that is taking place in Kashmir? Which General Roy Choudhury, at one point of time, categorically called it the Fourth Indo-Pak War? If it has done so, it is good, but is it the indication of the way forward ?. I will never say that we do not need army aviation, but I will say that the concept of army aviation has be taken as part and parcel of national airpower. It is an important consideration and we need a deeper analysis. We need to develop future concept of operations.

Having said this, may I make a few suggestions? Army aviation alone is not good enough. There is a requirement and there is an inflexible interrelationship of different air operations of war -all supportive of each other. Airspace management is not just a term, it is an important ingredient and when one talks about the expansion of army aviation, let us also consider that there will be a few more problems of airspace management and these must come through. There will be a difficulty in terms of ground defence and AD, large dispersion of forces, based on operational plans that we have seen, being enunciated today. There will be the cost factor and I think any other option which may reduce the cost without markedly reducing the capabilities, need to be addressed.

USA is a different cup of tea. The system of the USA is that we will create the air superiority, then you go ahead and do what you have to. We cannot afford their numbers and when air superiority cannot be guaranteed, I think sytem of control is more important than ownership.

In Israel, all air assets are under a single command. Somebody mentioned that it's an army General, but I read in one of these recent *Jane's Weekly* to say that the next Chief of Staff of IDF is an air force officer. In other words the need for unity is everywhere. The more parochial we get in our individual services, the more harm we are doing to ourselves individually and to the armed forces. In UK, all helicopters are under one command. Why? Because I think this dual-tasking ability gives us better for less money or greater capability for the same amount of money. Please appreciate that the requirement does not become equal everywhere and we cannot always talk in terms of best case scenario. We need to keep things under control.

Regarding the ownership of attack helicopters by the army, I can only say that till we get a full system of control, let us please remember this that there has to be some integration between attack helicopters or armed helicopters and fighter aircrafts. On this issue, I am willing to place my professional reputation on the platter. It was necessary during Kargil, it is necessary everywhere else. What are the various systems that we have introduced to achieve it? What are the organisations that we have raised? These are the factors that need mulling over.

If the army aviation wants those (attack) helicopters, please apply and let the services debate this. But, remember there will always be a need of an integrated approach of fighter aircrafts and helicopters.

Air OP role and airborne command posts; I think these are passé today. Today we are speaking about exercising command from anywhere on earth or in space. And here we are advocating to use these helicopters for the purpose like this. I do not think it is valid. What is needed is the UAV, that will give surveillance that you need immediately, within those 3-4 miles that you have, which is going to grow with the affordability of technology.

Modernisation of thoughts is essential, we have mini-UAVs today, and micro UAVs are coming up. An UAV can get you situational awareness much faster and during the thick of battle when you cannot risk sending an aircraft or a helicopter. We all understand there are needs of LICO and CI operations. Can this seriously be done without UAVs, without ground troops, without helicopters and without space assets? I do not think so. So when we discuss their utilisation in LICO and anti-terrorist operations, let us understand that we will need more things like UAVs.

I was rather surprised that under the guise of army aviation the word UAV has not been spoken of today. To me it (UAV) is the way forward. Now, as to how good these (UAVs) are? An American experience from Kosovo, I have taken it from a report. I quote, "Very early in the conflict, General Clarke requested for deployment of AH-64 Apache helicopters. This was not recommended by the air component commander, who said that over here these helicopters will not do the trick. General Clarke insisted. As per the Rand report, the deployment of the two battalions of Apache, 24 helicopters in all, was accompanied by 26 UH-60 Black Hawk, CH-47 Chinook, a light infantry company, a MLRS platoon, an anti-tank company with 38 utility vehicles, an intelligence platoon, a military police platoon, a combat service support team, a mechnised infantry company with 14 Bradley AFVs, an armour company with 15 M1 A2 Abram tanks, a howitzer battery with eight 155 mm artillery pieces, a construction engineer company, a short range AD battery with eight more Bradley AFVs, a smoke generator platoon, a brigade headquarters compliment and much more. In all, the 24 attack helicopters were accompanied by 5,350 army personnel. Unquote. The large supporting force was possibly needed because they were operating away from the rest of the army in that area. Granted, but the support required for the ground defence needs and the AD needs cannot be understated. It will be required. Well, they (Apache Battalions) went there, the cost of deployment was $ 254 million, which is equal to eight per cent of total cost of Kosovo conflict. Inspite of all this expenditure, the Serbian AD were perceived as 'effective and up', prohibiting the offensive use of helicopters. Not one combat mission was flown but two helicopters crashed during training and non-operational sorties. In the words of General Shelton, the then chief of the joint chiefs of staff: "The anticipated benefits of employing the Apaches against the dispersed forces in a high threat environment did not outweigh the risks to our pilots." This happened only six years ago and I think the requirement and the need for us is to understand, that there is a problem called 'vulnerability' even for the Americans who are using Apaches, which is so much better than any thing else that we have. Let us examine the Iraqi conflict, in an attack against the Republican Guard Division, the (US) used 30 Apache helicopters. All of them returned to base with injuries. They were all damaged. Can we afford these things? Please sit back and consider.

Pakistan has got 400 aeroplanes we were told, do they deter us in any way? It is not the numbers that is important, it is the method of resource utilisation which is important. I think that there is a serious thinking needed on our requirement. 'Best' will always be the enemy of the 'good'. Let us decide as to what we require to be able to match those capabilities. Thereafter, we can decide up on organisational and such like issues.

I was very impressed with what General Oberoi said this morning about the motto of the Centre for Land Warfare Studies "Victory Through Vision." In consonance with this particular motto, may I end by quoting from Alvin Tofler, " The illiterate of the 21st century will not be those who cannot read and write but those who can not learn, unlearn and relearn." May I say that I fully agree with Alvin Tofler in this regard and I commend this wisdom to all present here today?

Lieutenant General Shankar Prasad

With your permission sir, I do not wish to reply to Air Marshal Patney because he and I have been working together for the last so many years. I recall when I was Major General General Staff, Northern Command and he was Air Officer Commanding (J&K) and we used to work together.

Gentlemen, we have been through some very interesting papers this morning. We have got enough knowledge available to us from developed countries and their armed forces, particularly relating to the army aviation. While it is important and necessary to know the details of those countries and their army aviation, but I think the armed forces of India must realistically look at the current local security environment. Our threat perception and response has been articulate many times this morning, but just to put them in perspective we need to know who are the principle enemies that we are going to combat today? What is the status of our nuclear capability? Where is insurgency taking us? It has been on our hands for a long time now. We have not been able to find a good answer or a resolution to this problem. What is the kind of duration of wars that we are going to fight in the future? What is the kind of destruction that we are capable of inflicting on the enemy? Or the enemy is capable of inflicting on us, before the nations go nuclear. Is insurgency the only way we are going to carry on? Is there going to be a window of opportunity to wage a small-scale conventional war before it escalates to bigger issues.

If we put all these things together and try to answer them, the answer is known to all of us. The biggest problem that we have been facing and continue to face is the insurgency in many of our states. It is really costing us dearly, and we are trying to combat it for last so many years. There is a need to improve our capability to fight this better. To this audience I do not have to give a detailed presentation but suffice to say very briefly, if we were able to locate and destroy the terrorists camps across the LoC, perhaps it will be a quantum jump in our capability. We have the SF which is trained equipped and well-led but have we got the resources to really utilize them. If we had a helicopter resource or an air resource where we could use the SF, may be we would have had a great success in CI operations.

We are going to face short-duration, not so deep penetrating strategic manoeuvres and conventional wars where we need to get quick results, yet not cross the nuclear threshold. In that, our strike corps or pivot crops would need very intimate support of rotary or fixed wing aircrafts. To put it simply the army needs our reconnaissance capability, utility capability and attack capability.

Admiral Menon felt that the resources are going to be dished out the way air force does, I am afraid, it is not going to be really like that. The army has a set pattern of developing an operational plan. It all begins at the command headquarters, goes down to the corps headquarters with specific mission and specific tasking and therefore specific allocation of certain resources. Some resources which are available could be given to the divisions and corps, the ones which are hard to get could be centrally controlled at the level of command. Some other resources which are absolutely necessary are allocated to the corps and at times to the divisions. But that does not mean that you are dishing out the resources and that is the end of the matter. It is the development of an integrated plan for an operational reason with specific goal in mind. Therefore, for me to go on saying that the army aviation needs to be more integrated in to the army is something that I need not to say anymore. But what I like to say is a comment on what Admiral Menon said about army aviators, negative response to the questions that he had asked. I must tell you that I have asked these questions ever since I read his paper to some of the aviators and they were aghast to learn about his script, Raja I do not know whom you spoke to but I am actually surprised to hear this. I checked it with the aviators of today of the rank of majors, colonels and brigadiers and they were completely dazed to hear the answers and they wanted to read the paper. Gentlemen, it is really not so . I think the army aviation is a forward-looking organisation, there are some problems. I am not suggesting that army aviation as it exists, today is flawless. There is a certain amount of integration required within the service. There is a requirement of further studies and conceptualisation of plans. There is a lot of haziness in this present set up. It is also true that the hierarchy in army headquarters is not giving clear direction. But the fact of the matter is that the army aviation has to be part of Indian Army in tackling conventional and sub-conventional conflicts. The important point is that we have to train our leaders to be able to understand the capabilities of army aviation. That element in the army is somewhat lacking. I retired about two years ago and not much would have changed in these two years. But it is true for me to say that there is a lack of perception amongst the commanders about the capabilities of army aviation, when they have to employ helicopters for reconnaissance, utility and attack tasks.

Gentlemen, whenever we discuss army aviation the issue tends to get rather emotional, and because it creates, so much emotion, we tend to lose the focus. Therefore, I very strongly recommend to shed these emotions and evaluate the role of army aviation in the light of role and tasks of the field formations of the army.

Vice Admiral S.C. Chopra

Now we have heard the three speakers who have covered for you a number of air forces and armies who run the army aviation in the manner they do so. I wish to pass one or two comments because they have come during the proceedings and Lieutenant General Prasad did not pick it up. I am going to say something to Air Marshal Patney's comment about the two squadrons of Apache, which arrived in Kosovo and did nothing. That is true, but a number of fighter squadrons which arrived there flew about 5,000 sorties, dropped 14,000 tons of ammunition and also did nothing. Because the Yugoslavs were too clever for them. The fighter aircrafts were employed to destroy Serbian armoured and mechanised forces, but it remained unscathed. Damage was inflicted on the civilian targets, such as buildings and bridges. In other words, they (pilots) went for their weekly sorties to practice bombing. But the result of Kosovo was that Serbian will to fight was broken despite their armed forces being intact. Before I open the house for discussion I want to make another point. What is emerging from the presentations and comments is that it is for the army to make up their mind what they want to do. What other armies are doing can only serve as a pointer. It is your own will to decide that you need attack helicopters, assault helicopters and tactical transport helicopters. If that be so then you have to shed some of your own flab. It was the same argument, which we used to have in naval headquarters 30 years ago. You could not say that I will also have the gun and I also want an aircraft. You can say that you will have massive anti-submarine warfare (AWS) equipment on-board and also a helicopter, which does the same job. A direct and distinct choice has to be made. I often wonder as to why army wants to maintain such a large mule train to stock up forward areas in the mountains. A fleet of helicopters will do that in two weeks, which is done in six months by mules. There is an entrenched lobby within the army headquarters, which wants the mules to remain. Similarly, there is an entrenched lobby, which opposes expansion of aviation corps.

Lieutenant Colonel Jaswant Singh

I have an observation on employment of attack helicopters in Kosovo operations. Average, night-flying experience of pilot was five hours. The squadron commanders had about 25-30 hours on Apache and a few had none. On an average, the pilots had five hours of night-flying experience. They could not just take off. The two aircrafts that took off at night, their pilots had less than five hours average and that's why the accidents took place. So that is one of the reasons, the Apaches never took off at night.

Air Marshal Vinod Patney

No, I think Jaswant's point needs some clarification. I am not saying that they (Apaches) did not fly or the fighter aircrafts were able to do so much more. The fact of the matter is that well camouflaged army targets are difficult to hit. It is because of this reason American said they will need attack helicopters. General Wesley Clarke was so much in favour of employing these against the army tanks. In the event they did not do it, because General Shelton, another army general turned around and said that Serbian air defences were too strong for employing attack helicopters. In fact, Serbian air defences at that time were in disarray. So what I am trying to say is that there is a vulnerability quotient, which we should understand. I am not decrying that the Apaches did not fly. I am saying that there is a requirement to deal with the (air defences) and when these air defence are active the helicopters are vulnerable.

Commander Negi

Sir, I am from naval operations directorate and a naval aviator myself. I have a small question for Air Marshal Patney. To me it seems that we are discussing that whether some elements of air power should be with the army or air force. The fact of the matter is that today, aircrafts or helicopters are ubiquitous. Everyone nowadays owns a helicopter. There is nothing special in this machine which takes to the air, that it should be counted towards the national air power. To us in the navy it is unthinkable to plan any operation without dedicated air support. First naval unit during a manoeuvres is a maritime reconnaissance aircraft, last to leave is a MR aircraft in between if the captain of the ship has to do a ASW hunter-killer mission, he employs his helicopter either with sonar or with a weapon or he borrows a helicopter. So it is completely integrated. May I suggest that we should look at the helicopter as a flying weapons platform, it could be with the army or with any other service.

Air Marshal Vinod Patney

Not for a moment did I say where it (helicopter) should be? When I speak about national air power, I am afraid that every single machine that takes to the air is part of national air power. Its tasking can be changed, depending on the requirement and there is also the problem of airspace management. The more number of helicopters we have, more problems will crop in. I am only saying that if you could prove to the powers that be that you need three times more helicopters that you already have, best of luck to you. I am suggesting to you that while you put up this case, just remember factors, like airspace management, air defence and ground defence can not be ignored. As far as who should own it my answer is let us talk in terms of capabilities first. That is where national air power capabilities come in.

Next question! How are we going to utilise these capabilities. What is the purpose that we require these for? What are the capabilities that we want and it is tertiary in my opinion as to who controls it and who runs it. What is important is that what is needed and the calculation of the requirement must be on the basis of prioritisation.

Major General Atma Singh

Sir, my question is for Air Marsahl Patney. Actually, this discussion I thought was to have a look at army aviation in 2025, but some of the arguments have taken me back 30 years on to 1975. When General Raina had prepared a very strong case, that was first time that such a paper was presented to a committee, formed by defence minister to study the need of army aviation. It consisted of defence secretary, cabinet secretary and principle secretary to the prime minister. The projections made by army three decades ago have come alive today. When all these debates were going on in the foreign countries, in the USA somebody defined the helicopter like this, " Helicopter is a ground vehicle which moves without contact with the ground." I quoted this in School of Land Air Warfare, where a senior air force officer was lecturing. He said, "No, it an aerial vehicle." Now about the airspace management, I just want to ask who controls about hundred feet of airspace above ground in a brigade, division and corps? Certainly not the air force.

Next, the integration of attack helicopters, I think they need integration with the tanks, tank hunting teams and the ATGMs in the area and not with the close air support. Time does not allow further elucidation of this (argument), but it is my view point.

Air Marshal Vinod Patney

Airspace management is by definition, the job and task of a agency, you want to get it done by the civilians, get it done by the civilians. But it has to be a single agency. After all there are enemy aircraft also involved and whether it is 100 feet off the ground or not, can you legislate to the enemy that you shall not fly below 100 feet? There are other aircrafts that are moving around. This is a local arrangement that we get to because our communication systems are not so good. Army to fly below 100 feet so that air force knows that any thing below 100 feet is a friendly aircraft.

On the other hand, suppose there is an enemy aircraft below 100 feet. Under those circumstances we would not even know. Hence, as our communication systems improve, we are telling to army that inform us as to where each of those airborne objects go. In fact we need to know when the artillery is firing or any other air defence aspect is coming in. Airspace management is something far greater than what you are thinking of at present. And, I am saying that it has to be a single agency. It cannot be too many people but if you insist on saying that the helicopter is a ground vehicle without touching the ground, then I have nothing to comment on.

Unidentified Speaker

Sir, what we are mixing up is a policy for airspace management versus control of weapon system being employed in that area. When you formulate policies at the national level or between the three services, air space management will be a deciding factor. But when it comes to the ground forces commanders, who have to implement that policy and weapon systems that are going to be employed within that space then there will be too many people to control the weapon systems. Then one agency cannot control it. Telling a brigade commander that he cannot fire his guns and other weapon systems in his areas of influence will have a different connotation. A system of control whether it is vertical, horizontal or timed is needed. So, I do not think that Air Marshal means that every body will start controlling the airspace, it is about controlling the weapon systems in a particular area.

Vice Admiral S.C. Chopra

What the Air Marshal perhaps means that these are the kind of roadblocks you will meet in your proposal. Because the air force will always bring a red herring.

Air Marshal Vinod Patney

Yes. These are the roadblocks that army should be able to deal with before you make your proposal. Because these are the requirements which will have to be dealt with, not because of air force. Air force roadblocks don't interest me at present, what interest me is capability.

Colonel U.S. Rathore

Sir, it was brought out that the firepower and mobility are key battle winning factors. It is the army aviation with its inherent capabilities which can maximise these for a force commander. A strike corps, unless it has inherent and integrated air power, it cannot achieve its objectives. There is no doubt in anybody's mind that the capability of a land force commander will be greatly enhanced if the army aviation is made more potent.

Having heard so many speakers today, I doubt that Army's proposals will ever fructify unless there is a road map. These plans have been on the anvil for so many years but nothing has happened. We need to sensitise our hierarchy - army, sister services, MoD and civilians. Unfortunately, decision makers are left out of the loop. We discuss the issue amongst ourselves and put forward ground recommendation, which do not see the light of the day.

Therefore, we got to be very clear within the Army regarding the doctrine, approach, requirement and structures. Thereafter sensitise the environment in various forums so that the proposal moves forward in the hierarchy with favorable recommendation. Thank you.

Lieutenant General V.K. Nayyar

I am not really raising a question but I want to put across one or two points. I think it is now established that the AAC is here to stay. So, it is futile to question its existence. Presently, I have noticed between the army and the air force, there is a growing understanding of each other's problems, which, I think had reached a high level during World War II. I will quote Air Marshal Cunnigham who was Chief of Air Support of the Eighth Army, when he wrote to Montgomery that, "I want to share the headquarters and the stool in your mess, sleep on the same ground sheet where you people stay and not go thirty miles away in the cool climate of Mediterranean where you want my air headquarters to exist. Because unless we sit together drinking the same cup of tea in the same situation, there will always be a gap in our thinking and the air force may not be able to give you the desired support." Let me tell you the Eighth Army had an excellent air support due to this perfect liaison and understanding of each other. Now once the AAC expands its tasks will be basically SF operations, CI operations and support to the troops in the front line. Unless the people live together in the same geographical area and know each other individually, intimate support in the tactical battle area will not be possible. In this regard the helicopters have an advantage over the fighter aircraft as the helipads and mounting bases can be made in close proximity of headquarters and units. Hence, cohesion of helicopter units and the pilots, with the users could be greater and fruitful - sharing the success and failure together. The tasks that I see for army aviation are of 'quick works' type, if the helicopters have to come from a far off distance, they will be unaware of the area, terrain and most importantly - the commanders and that will affect the cohesion, which is very important for the success of a mission.

The Air Marshal talking to us earlier over a cup of tea, he is a supporter of the AAC, but there are reservations, which will get sorted out once the AAC starts functioning in its expanded form.

Commodore Ranjit B Rai

Sir, though this session is meant for discussing the foreign army aviation structures, but it has transgressed into what the Indian Army's Aviation Corps is today. Therefore my question is to Air Marshal Patney and Lieutenant General Sihota and Lieutenant General Shankar Prasad. As a naval officer I understand two things and if I am wrong please correct me. First, the command of the attack helicopters and of course other helicopters, which support the army, is with the air force. Air force hands over control to the army as and when required. If my understanding is correct at the present moment then my question will continue. Second, the attack helicopters are funded from the budget of the army and if that understanding is also correct then I shall proceed with my question. But I will not proceed with the question if the understanding that I am under with Indian Army is incorrect. If you could answer those I shall ask two very pertinent questions.

The question therefore is the army has to ask to itself, has it worked? I recollect that during 1965 war, the navy had a big problem on this. Today, I see two Generals, one Admiral and one Air Marshal tell us we are emotional people. The cultural aspects of the nature of operations is to be taken in to account. The second thing, we have been told that the funds are a constraint and therefore, though I congratulate the IAF for having done a fantastic job; some of you must have read, that they rescued Pakistanis in Congo and saved them. It has been a magnificent operation some ten days ago by the IAF. Regarding the command

and control, I would pose a question to the Generals, when we talk about national airspace of course the command is with the air force, no matter how emotional we get anything that happens in the country must be cleared by the air force, other wise it will be a national security risk.

If we take it to command and control (of attack helecopter) then the air force has to be absolutely generous and say these squadrons now belong to the army. The control is also with the army and the part of (their) command. I would just like to ask whether this is possible and whether in the past this command and control has worked or not. The navy found it very difficult and in 1965 war we were let down because we had Liberators. Even today we have Jaguars, which are in support for strike at sea with Sea Eagle missile. In 1965 war, when we tried to do something in navy, the Liberators were flying from Poona escorting merchant ships as war ships. Two such operations were conducted and therefore the MoD told that navy is not aware of the situation at sea. We had to send officers including me on board of Liberators to tell that navigator - in navy we call them observers, literally teaching him in the midst of war about the difference between merchant ship and war ship. Therefore, my honest question to Air Marshal Patney is in Indian context with limited resource, limited budget in the short-term, can somebody else have command and somebody else have control. In the long-term, we will see what happens whether it is UAV or helicopters. We have not even come to the conclusion whether we should call these machines helos or the hepters.

Air Marshal Vinod Patney

As far as your Liberator analogy is concerned, all I can say is that much of that training and explanation that you are giving should have been done before the war. The fact that we are not very good in preparing for the next war is pretty obvious and some of the questions that have been raised and the concept that has been enunciated this morning gives me the impression that we are not very good in preparing for the next war. In fact we are not very good at all. This includes me as well. Command of attack helicopters was done so many years ago on the basis of a few points that I remember. One, combat flying requires training with combat pilots including fighter pilots. Two, combat flying is not something that you do for a short period of time and then forget it, particularly if the total number of aircrafts, that one has is limited. Then you cannot create a combat pilot cadre in the army. Hence, it was said that it will be that much better. All these were important considerations, which at that particular point in time were agreed by army and I think for very good reason. Last point that I must make is that as I mentioned to you and I will say it again that I will put my professional reputation on platter, when I make this assumption that today, to be able to deal with the attack helicopters on its own is a fallacy. It would be incorrect to do so because you cannot carryout a single aeroplane attack. The aircraft that you are operating is a part of a very large system. A word about the utilisation of air power, if I am unable to explain it to you, it is because you do not have first hand experience. On this issue please take what I say as gospel (truth).

Air Commodore Jasjit Singh

The understanding between the two chiefs on attack helicopters was what it is now. It was also agreed that a common cadre of pilots from the army and air force will exist so that at a future date it will be a cadre of combat pilots from Indian Army and by the same logic it was agreed in the same agreement that such officers who are seconded to the army from the air force or from air force helicopters, they will have equal opportunity to become the chief of a different service to which they belonged.

Lieutenant General Shankar Prasad

These were the compromises, which were made at the time of raising of army aviation. I do not agree with the Air Marshal on one issue that a fighter aircraft pilot and attack helicopter pilot are the same. I am afraid these two are totally different. I will give you a live example from exercise Vijay Chakra, in which I commanded a corps. During the manoeuvers, the helicopters flew in from their bases located 100-150 km away to support the ground troops for which FAARPs were established. When the helicopters landed there they only had ten minutes' endurance left to engage the targets. That is the issue. The air force does not understand this problem, helicopters will arrive on demand but would ask for refueling for which ten browsers were needed. That is where integration is becoming more and more essential, which can only come about if the attack helicopters are a part and parcel of the formation headquarters to which it is actually going to support.

Brigadier Chauhan

The first attack helicopter squadron was raised by a helicopter pilot Group Captain RB Singh, who never flew fighters. So, to say that the attack helicopters must be flown by fighter pilots and they must be regularly reverted back to fighter pilot duties is not being followed by the air force.

Air Marshal Vinod Patney

Permit me to interrupt you. No body is saying that fighter pilots need to fly attack helicopters. I said that in case there is somebody who has flown fighter aircraft he is better suited, but far more importantly, you need to train attack helicopter pilots in combat environment and that includes flying of fighter aircrafts. Many of our attack helicopter pilots go to Jamnagar and Bangalore where they train together with tactics and concept development establishment. These are the nuances which are proved. It is not just business of flying from place A to place B and landing. It is much more than that.

Brigadier Chauhan

Sir, you did not let me complete. I was bringing out what time and again has been debated. At present, for carrying out joint training of attack helicopters or hellborne operations the army has to send a requisition two months in advance, hold the meeting (with air force) one month in advance other wise they (the helicopters) do not show up. So I just want to say if this is the method of liaison and coordination, army needs them (the helicopters) or not.

Lieutenant General S.J.S Saigal

I wish to comment upon what Air Commodore Jasjit has said, referring to an agreement which is twenty years old now. The operational requirements of the army have changed tremendously and so are tasks of its formations. It would be incorrect to cite a two-decade old agreement for maintaining the status quo.

Brigadier Shandil

Sir, I am Commandant of the Combat Army Aviation Training School being raised at Nasik. I have a few comments. We are projecting our ideas, with a view to protect own turfs. I am constrained to observe that the Air Marshal has been singled out because of numbers. There is no scope of dispute as far as the command essentials are concerned. It is clear that there is a need for totally integrated force structure and integrated staff. The best man to command these forces is the one who is responsible for the out come of the battle on the ground. The resources thus should be placed under his command. Will that be acceptable to the air force? Certainly not. As the air force only want to do the task and not be placed under command. That is also a school of thought, but that is not desirable under the changed operational situations. Why all countries, Western or Eastern, have developed their army aviation, it could lead us to find an answer to our dispute.

The attack helicopters are not for close air support. There are an extension of the fire support from the ground and close air support with fixed wing aircraft is best left to the air force.

The helicopter pilots all over the world are being trained directly on to helicopters; there is no duality in their training, be it the British or French armies I have visited both.

Rear Admiral K. Raja Menon

Low intensity operations started in 1989, 16 years have passed and in these 16 years the army aviation has not played a decisive role. In Kargil conflict the army aviation did not play a decisive role. If the army had a different approach to army aviation, Operation Parakram would not have happened the way it did.

No political leader is going to give you permission to launch three strike corps across the other side to teach Pakistan a lesson.

Army aviation therefore needs a separate approach. On the other hand there has to be an acceptance of air force sensitivity and therefore there must be certain red lines. Army must not threaten the air force in its role in strategic air lift. You have no business there. You do not encroach on the common user fixed-wing aviation like the AN-32. You should not threaten the air force in the strategic arena.

The air force must understand that the army has certain red lines too. The SF helicopters have got to be with the army, not with the corps commander but with the SF commander. Battlefield helicopters - both attack and lift should be with the army. Battlefield reconnaissance and EW should be with the army. There are certain grey areas in between and that includes armoured fixed-wing ground support gunships. Command of air force fixed-wing assets should be with a single commander if the operations are conducted abroad or in continental India. These grey areas can be managed, but the red lines must be respected. I think then there will be peace.

Lieutenant General Shankar Prasad

I have only one comment to what Raja Menon has said. Earlier, during his presentation he had made a remark that air force is scared about the open-ended expansion of army aviation. Now he has categorised the respective fields of operations of the army aviation and air force. Therefore, army's vision of its aviation corps is not open ended, it is with in certain parameters. Army is not thinking about owning medium and heavy lift fixed-wing aircrafts. Hence, there is no reason for air force to feel threatened.

Vice Admiral S.C. Chopra

Let me sum up the session. I will narrate to you the naval experience. Navy has been interacting with the air force for the last fifty years and on most of the occasion I have been associated with the subject. In the early Fifties the navy was run by gunnery officers and these officers wanted a target to train their crews on. The only people who could provide a target was the air force. And navy had to ask for the air force's participation two months in advance. If, in between one letter did not go, air force would not turn up and the fleet sailed, there were ships at sea but the aircraft did not arrive. So therefore, to get rid of the problem, the first unit that was created in the navy was "Fleet Requirement Unit." We bought ten Sea Lands, slow as they may be but they trained our gunnery crew. My advice to army is not to blame air force but think of ways and means to obtain their co-operation and participation. You got to establish a need for an attack helicopter or assault helicopter supporting your forward troops. Air force has to yield eventually. That's what happened to naval aviation fifty years ago. Army headquarters has to do much more thorough homework. The need for battlefield helicopter is to be justified by the army alone and no other service will do it for you.

General V.N. Sharma

It was a good discussion and I enjoyed listening to everybody. The first thing that I want to say is that the services should be clear about the type of helicopter they need. I think the HAL-produced ALH fits the bill for every service. It would be pragmatic to base our future requirements on this machine. Services can sit together and decide on General Staff Qualitative Requirements (GSQRs) and give that to DRDO/HAL. Today, any aircraft in the battle zone has to be armed, immune to small arms fire to certain degree and equipped with on-board sensors and equipment that enable it to fly and fight at night. An unarmed helicopter in the battle field has no survivalability.

The IAF is responsible for the airspace and military flying in our country. Therefore, the air force has to be quite convinced about the requirements and demands of the army. So, if the air force is convinced and supportive of army's case it will get through much faster. Opposition from air force will give a chance to the bureaucracy to turn down army's proposal, no matter how good or deserving it is.

Army should not go in for creating a big organisation right from the start. To begin with, it would be prudent to raise couple of smaller organisations and validate them in the exercises and improve upon. I think Air Marshal Patney had a point where he said that in the plains sector where we do not foresee deep penetrations due to many reasons, organisation like aviation brigades for armoured division will serve little purpose. Example of USA is different, they have not operated against a strong enemy, hence, asymmetry does not throw up valid lessons for us to emulate. Their operations as a technological demonstrator are fine. Even in an environment of total air superiority in Iraq, the USA has lost a number of helicopters due to fire from non-air defence weapons. Helicopters are indeed vulnerable in the battlefield.

We have to take small steps. Many senior strike corps commanders, whom I know personally, have found it difficult to fathom how to use the armoured division on the ground. Let's be frank, six regiments of tanks and so many regiments of mechanised infantry, it is not easy to orchestrate their move in to concentration areas and across the border. It is a massive force to manage operationally.

I recall after the 1971 war, General Manekshaw, the then COAS came down to the headquarters of 1 Armoured Division and told us in the officers' mess, "You guys did not even go to the war." Everybody kept mum and I replied, "Sir, the armoured division is the mighty force of Richard -the Lion Heart. Do we have in the army Richard- the Lion Heart to lift this sword and use it"? So, the training for corps and army commanders to use armoured division and mechanised divisions is important.

Now, if you add an aviation brigade in to the ambit of the existing armoured divisions we will have to seriously look at the restructuring of their organisation. It cannot be an add on. An aviation brigade will off set certain elements from the armoured corps, the mechanised infantry, army air defence and even from the services. This would again need training of senior commanders.

I would be very happy to see the squadron leaders of the IAF and squadron commanders of the armoured corps doing tactical courses together. It is a must for forging better understanding. The idea of having tri-service institutions like National Defence Academy, DSSC, College of Defence Management and NDC is to forge inter-service understanding.

As far as army aviation's demands are concerned, it seems to me that their bottom line is that they want to have integral attack and airlift ability in a tactical battlefield. Even in CI operations like in Doda an infantry company or a platoon takes days and hours to reach an area where the militants are reported to be hiding. A few airlift helicopters owned by the army could have been very handy in such a situation.

So, the army's demand for self-reliance in troop airlift by using helicopters in a tactical battlefield scenario seems justified to me. Thank you.

Lieutenant General Vijay Oberoi

Well gentlemen, since I have the privilege of saying the 'last word', let me take a few moments on some issues which have come up for discussion today.

My first point is that the armed forces have to be ready for full spectrum warfare. That is what is contained in the doctrines of all the three Services. If that is the case, then we cannot legislate, what particular component is necessary or is absolutely unnecessary. What we need is a full spectrum capability and the army aviation also needs it. We also need to factor in the technology upgrades when we discuss structures of 2017 or 2025; but, unfortunately in the discussion I found that we tend to place the structures of tomorrow in the technology of today. That is why the 'gulf' between the two schools of thought exists.The resources will always be limited, but we have to find optimal solutions within these constraints.

The aim of the first session i.e. aviation structures of important countries was to learn lessons in doing and not doing certain things or in copying certain templates. What is more important is to use their experience to help us in affecting changes in our environment. Obiously, we have to be very judicious in decisions we take, but studying others does give us more ideas to look and probe.

Gentlemen, airpower is not just air force power and this is a point I have made earlier and I would like to make it again. What we need to reflect on is how the airpower can be optimally employed. This aspect was also addressed in some detail today but this may not take us very far, unless we agree to take a dispassionate view of the entire issue.

Sometimes I feel that the services tend to act like nation states. India is called status quo power and China, as a lot of people say, is an expansionist power. It seems to me that the air force wants the army to be a status quo power while they want to be like the Chinese, an expansionist power. I hope I am wrong.

Army and air force both need to grow and have a symbiotic relationship and not a confrontationist relationship between the two services. It seems to me that both the services have well-entrenched positions and they are not ready to budge on inch.

We need to change this, otherwise we will be paying only lip service to joint man ship and ultimately we would suffer in an ability to fight and win wars jointly.

In India, turf is important; as it is so in many countries, and it is not the case only with the services. In fact, you will be surprised how important it is in other departments and ministries and agencies in the government. Reason for this is only one -the paucity of resources. The inherent fear amongst the services is that gain of one is loss of the other. Why don't we look at it a little differently? It is not a zero-sum game. It is actually a function of doing the job as efficiently and as optimally as possible. Wars are fought by the armed forces and not by individual services. We have come a long way from the argument, where we were told in unambiguous terms that any thing that flies belongs to the air force. Things have now changed on both sides.

A point regarding the attack helicopters, whether it is a ground vehicle which flies or it gels best with the fighter aircraft are some arguments which may not find many takers in the army or in the air force. But I think the fact is that the attack helicopter has been designed as a 'flying tank'. It fights best with the tank men. Do not look at Mi-24, it was never an attack helicopter, it is a gunship. Unfortunately, we do not understand fully the difference between a gunship and an attack helicopter or an armed helicopter. We never had gunships which we need in LICO, where it would be very useful. The attack helicopter is a manoeuvre element, which could be a part of an armoured squadron /regiment /brigade. It is very much a component of the mechanised warfare. I think it is very wrong to say that there is no doctrine for employment of attack helicopters in the army. If there is no doctrine (which is incorrect), it is only because the armoured division and strike corps commanders do not get these helicopters when their formations are out on manoeuvres and exercises. And I am telling you this from my own experience of commanding an armoured division, a strike corps and later the Western Army.

A mention was made of composite unito. There is undoubtedly a great advantage of composite units. But there are disadvantages too and these are not just related to aviation, it is common to all other arms. There are systems that the armies have evolved; some have gone for integrated composite units while others haven't. There are good reasons for both.

Indian Army is certainly concerned with air superiority, I think Air Commodore Jasjit Singh mentioned about it. If you read Indian Army Doctrine-1998, there is a separate section on air superiority and favourable air situation and it is in the present doctrine too. So, it is incorrect to say that Indian Army does not believe in air superiority, I think it is our bread and butter. We believe in air superiority but the discussions over this issue get stalled on specious reasoning.

Gentlemen, the army cannot stand still while the air battle is going on -just waiting for air supremacy or favourable air situation to come about. Everyone who has spoken today has talked about short wars, intense wars and wars which would be over in a few days. War-waging needs initiative and concurrent offensive actions by all arms. Yet, we are talking about achieving air supremacy and favourable air situation in that graduated manner.

Of course, air superiority or favourable air situation is important. Between air force and the army it has to be decided as to how to achieve it. But to say that Indian Army does not think of it is incorrect thing to say.

In Session I, a point was mentioned about 'insatiable appetite' of army aviation when the 'open-ended' requirements of army aviation were talked about. The reality is that army aviation's growth plan is close-ended. Whenever army aviation thinks of integrating anything, it is looked at with great suspicion. Secondly, why should the vision of the army aviation not be open-ended? That's what visions are all about. It is the dynamics of the battlefield and the environment which change things and we must agree to that kind of open-endedness.

I am glad unity of command was mentioned. It is a very important issue, but why talk of it in isolation? We need it across the board and when it is offered (by army), it is not taken. But when it suits to a particular Service, it is mentioned.

Gentlemen, in the final analysis it boils down to the conduct of the land battle by the field commanders. They must have full wherewithal for the conduct of that battle under their command. A methodology has to be evolved for overcoming obstacles so that a joint mechanism is instituted. Thank you. ■

Pune Seminar:

Excerpts from Interactive Session

Admiral J.G. Nadkarni

The idea of AAC was mooted in 1963 and it took full 23 years before its implementation. Even after that, it has really stagnated for nearly 20 years. It started off with eight squadrons of light helicopters and today it just has 11 squadrons with no air combat capability and hardly any night (flying) capability. While we have stagnated or marked time, countries in the field of army aviation have progressed and evolved joint doctrines.

Major General Ashok Joshi

We must draw pragmatic conclusion about whether or not army aviation, as is understood by us today, and in the light of what we are likely to afford and have, is a full fledged combat arm. Is it one of a pair i.e. does it become a combat arm either operating with infantry or armoured corps or mechanised infantry or is it a combat arm on its own. We need to answer this basic question. Aviation structures of other armies could be of limited value as we have to develop our organisations based on our requirements.

Do we need strategic air mobility i.e. organic to Indian Army? If we do not, that will tell us whether we want fixed-wing aircraft as part of AAC. There could be instances where we need fixed-wing aircraft, for re-supply or cas evac but that does not justify inclusion of fixed-wing aircraft in the AAC.

What is the right mix of skill, knowledge and attitude which enables an aviator to perform his function? Is it the man whose sole purpose in life is to be an excellent flier or the man who can read the ground and ground battle? The air force has been arguing for many years that it is the principle business of a flier to be a flier and every other skill is secondary. This argument is self-serving. Very soon the AAC will be selling this argument to the army, if we aim for its open-ended growth.

The interesting point is that whenever any arm gets full-fledged combat, supporting and service elements, it separates itself into an independent service. In World War I, the Marine Corps branched off from US Navy and that has a lesson for us. If we, instead of having organic aerial platforms to perform multiple functions in support of land warfare, permit vertical and horizontal growth of AAC, it will soon become an aviation service. So we should be clear about what we want from this exercise.

Frankly, the role of Indian Armed Forces is subcontinental and not like the roles of armed forces of USA, UK, Germany and France. We have nothing to do with power projection capability.

From roles, one derives tasks, which are performed to fulfill those roles. Going backwards, one knows who performs these tasks to fulfill the roles. That is how an organisation should emerge. We cannot import the doctrine or equipment. I can tell you that when you import the equipment you also import the concepts and that is dangerous sign. There will always be arms producing nations encouraging us to buy weapons and equipment that we do not need. I wonder if US experience in Vietnam (regarding the employment of attack helicopter) is relevant at all because the US had to withdraw without achieving her political goal.

So when we decide on our requirements, I think we have to draw our own lessons. Similarly, drawing parallel with Pakistan Army Aviation is also incorrect. If we had three army generals as presidents (as in Pakistan), we too would have had a bigger aviation corps than Pakistan. So it is no logic. I do not know how many of you had a change to read Steve Cohen's book. He says about Pakistan, "After the Independence there was a British period, then an American period, now we have a Pakistan Army period." I hope India is not going backwards -the British period, Indian period and the US period.

I remember many years ago, one of the chiefs of IAF saying point-blank that in reality large proportion of IAF is tactical air force. The truth is what we must have organic to Indian Army and for what reason, is fundamental to what we have discussed so far. Major General Pitre rightly said (in his paper) that if India cannot produce the desired equipment, we will be forever importing our defence requirements. There is a strange relation between the technology which we use in our day to day life and the technology which we want to use in warfare. There cannot be a huge difference. The moment we opt for high-end technology, numbers of equipment procured is very small due to the prohibitive costs and it serves little purpose as one can not take losses.

Major General B.S. Pawar

Sir, the operational requirements of Indian Army are peculiar. Today actual operations are going on in the Northern Command and the AAC is heavily committed there. Our fliers are accomplishing these roles and tasks by using vintage helicopters, which are meant for light utility tasks. Their professionalism and doggedness is commendable.

We are looking for replacements; extensive trials are on and hopefully something will workout, which will enhance our capability in terms of troop lift, Casualty evacuation and stores carriage capability in all-terrain and all-weather conditions. In the ongoing CI operations, AAC's requirement is there, hence its demand for medium-lift helicopter is an operational imperative. There have been many occasions when troops could have achieved major success against the terrorists, if a detachment could be air-lifted and tactically deployed in the upper reaches of mountains to block their escape. Today one has to request the IAF through normal staff channel for a Mi-17 helicopter, which is time consuming and the opportunity slips away by the time the request materialises. Positioning of ALH in the Valley has really helped in achieving operational flexibility. This problem can be best addressed by providing medium-lift capability to AAC.

The attack helicopters may not be needed in CI operations, but in conventional war scenario these must be available with the corps commander as all battles will be fought at the level of a corps, hence a corps commander should have the ability to move troops and critical stores by helicopter with in a corps zone. It can only happen if the resources are organic to the corps.

Unidentified Speaker

Sir, what the three services need in terms of a helicopter, is an all-weather, all-terrain and medium-lift machine capable of day and night operation. Our Cheetah and Chetak helicopters are of sixties vintage, their lift capability is insignificant, which further goes down when these operate in places like Siachin. In fact these are meant for light communication duties and not for troops and cargo carriage.

Hence, we must replace these helicopters preferably with a common platform which can be suitably modified according to the need of the respective service.

Lieutenant General Ashok Kapoor

I had a chance to visit Russia, Poland, Czech Republic and some of the erstwhile Warsaw Pact countries in 2000. Their complete philosophy has changed after the breakup of the Soviet Union. In Russia, I found hundreds of helicopters standing lined up in the air fields with grass growing under their wheels. Lying unused as their conventional role has changed. Earlier, the artillery was a separate command in Russia, now Russians are trying to integrate everything together. Poland and Czech Republic also exchanged their aircrafts; Czech Republic took Mi-17 from Poland and gave their MiG-29s in return, as these countries were facing maintenance problems. Moreover, these countries were changing over to western models because of their inclusion in the NATO.

Russia does not intend fighting a major war anywhere. It has a problem with erstwhile Russian states only. So, the Russian example of fighting a conventional war and its template for AAC may not be entirely valid for us to emulate.

Air Commodore Ashok Bhaskar

I am a fighter pilot myself, but I have just come back from Leh after a two-year stint there. I have extensively flown the Cheetah helicopter in the Valley, right up to the Glacier. Just to allay the fear that it is a vintage aircraft, no doubt the design is of vintage, but let me assure you that every aircraft which flies in the Valley has got a brand new engine which is changed after every 200 hours of flying. The air frame is over hauled by the HAL after every 600 hours. The limitations of the aircraft are because of the density of air at those altitudes; its carriage capacity varies in winters and summers.

The aircraft may be of vintage but the IAF and AAC are doing yeoman service and sustaining even a lone soldier at 22,000 feet at Amar and Sonam picquets at the Glacier.

So, let us not put the fear in the pilots, the aircrafts are still airworthy and still a potent force, which is sustaining the troops at the Glacier. These aircrafts are also flying at night in the valley.

Major General B.S. Pawar

The AAC operates maximum number of Cheetah and Chetak helicopters in Siachin. There is no doubt that it is a vintage aircraft and you cannot equate it with the helicopters available today, which can operate at the same height with much better efficiency.

There is nothing to fear. All procedures are followed and timely overhauls are done, but the airframe and the gear box remains the same. These are two main restricting factors which do not permit an overhauled engine to perform. We may do everything else but these two handicaps will remain. In the last three years we have had forty cases of cracks in the air frame and one of them a fatal accident. So the ground realities cannot be wished away.

As far as the night-vision capability is concerned, we have now got second generation night-vision goggles in limited numbers. But the ALH is capable of flying at night depending upon the phases of the moon anywhere in the country.

The night-vision and avionics of Cheetah and Chetak do not match, so unlike the ALH these helicopters cannot be used for night operations.

Lieutenant General A. Mukherjee

I would like to make an observation on the employment of attack helicopters as envisioned by us as well as the future requirements, as vertical projection of the manoeuvre arm, particularly operating with mechanised forces in offensive operations.

Much of our concepts as brought out by some of the speakers have been sold to us by the Americans and they carried out trials when the first attack helicopter emerged in the form of AH-64 Apache under NATO conditions in the early eighties. It was a great sales pitch, and when they (the Americans) war gamed these machines vis-à-vis' the simulated Russian armour they came out with certain kill ratios.

Lieutenant General H.M. Khanna

I was a young officer in 1961, commissioned in to 8th Light Cavalry. I did my young officers' course and would have got the young officer trophy, but for what I wrote as a paper of a future battle tank. I opined that the future battle tanks will be lightly armoured, capable of firing missiles, and will fly over obstacles. Everybody ridiculed me for this paper and called it the flight of imagination. That was in 1961.

Today that figment of imagination has come true in the form of attack helicopters.

The role the AAC is confined to R&O and all it owns is light helicopters of sixties' vintage. The theme of the seminar is RRO i.e. reorganisation, revitalisation and optimisation. I suggest you add another 'R' to it, i.e. reality check.

The presentations have suggested reorganisation of AAC of two extremes -one, money is not a consideration; secondly, where the money is going to come from?

Here a reality check is needed: Funds and financial implications are important but one should not get hamstrung by it. In such a situation institutional resistance is also important, which has always advocated status quo. This seminar is a very good idea to make the system pay heed to your point of view.

Sadly, in our context, we pay lip service to the idea of jointmanship and all services are to be blamed for it.

Air is the most important single element today to determine the outcome of land battle. The eternal question in our context is which aspects should be controlled by the IAF and which one should be looked after by the Army.

The IAF has graduated in to an aerospace power and according to me it operates in the strategic domain. Tactical lift and tank busting from the IAFs point of view are the least priority task and it needs to be delegated to Army. The Army, as opposed to Air Force, essentially operates in the tactical domain and it wins battle by manoeuvres, where the air plays a decisive role. The Army cannot be left dependent on others for its decisive elements. Hence, all resources employed in a tactical battle area should be controlled and be integral to the Army. The environment of the tactical battle is shaped by the Air Force and therefore, the overlapping roles in the tactical area are - the Air force shapes the environment and the Army fights the tactical battle. If one keeps these factors in mind, I think the deadlock can be resolved. Roles of each service in war are well demarcated and we have not progressed beyond that point. Jointmanship has been reduced to mere jargon. The spirit of jointmanship gets eclipsed by personalities and institutions. Permit me to quote an example. I and one Air Marshal are course mates from our RIMC days and we served together in London. So, you cannot blame us as individuals. On 13 May 1999 in Kargil, the station commander Air Force, on realising the gravity of the situation suggested that AN-32s could be used for bombing the enemy's stronghold. So, I asked the staff officers to bid for air support. Air Force declined by citing that use of Air Force could escalate the conflict. It was only on 25 May that the first air sortie was sanctioned. By this time the enemy had brought in the SAMs and you know what happened on the next day.

Air Force did a good job that too in the mountains; Muntho Dhalo was knocked out in a pinpoint attack. So, I would wrap up by saying that the Army should have medium-lift and attack helicopters with it. UAVs should be integrated (to AAC). But, I agree with Admiral Kulkarni that the present attack helicopters - the Mi-35 (Akbar) is not worth inheriting. So, do not press for this one. Let the IAF procure a new one and then start a campaign for its transfer to the Army.

Air Marshal Kulkarni

I would start first by thanking the Centre for Land Warfare Studies for giving me the opportunity to read the approach paper and other papers to give my comments. Of course, the IAF has been on the block since morning.

The Admiral talked about the resources and I would not agree with those who say that, "the resources would not be a problem, plan whatever you like and these will be made available" this type of optimism will not work.

This caution is because of my own experience, when I was doing a project on the programme budgeting for the Armed Forces. The first Director General Defence Planning Staff, Lieutenant General B.C. Nanda told me that the three services were looking differently at the future and their long-term plans were different and there was no meeting ground between them. Of course that (situation) continues even today. Lieutenant General Nanda said that he was going to the COAS to the discuss the next plan and asked me to join him. When we met the COAS, he talked about his vision which included the Army acquiring 3,000-4,000 helicopters by next plan. Lieutenant General Nanda asked the COAS, "Sir, where would money come from?" The COAS had no answer. The same COAS wrote a paper which talked about acquiring 2,000 helicopters by the year 2000. It is already 2006 and the Army has not been able to upgrade its existing fleet of helicopters. I feel bad for the Army, it should not have happened. But the resource crunch is for real and we should accept it.

Let us go back to 1991-96 when the defence budget of the country was brought down from 3.6 per cent to 2.6 per cent of the GDP to cut the fiscal deficit by the same people who are at the helms today. The point I am making it is that there is no lack of vision but the vision without resources is of no use. These two must be matched to sustain a growth plan.

Even today there is a lot of stress to restrict defence budget to around 2.5 per cent of the GDP which in real terms, would amount to reduction in the allotment. It has adversely affected the R&D and yet we talk about indigenisation. I admire the services for what they have achieved despite subsisting on a 'shoe-string budget'.

We still do not have a jet engine with us and that is a reality. The tone and tenor of the proceedings so far, prompt me to think that it is indeed an exercise to draft a proposal to create a full fledged tactical Air Force as a combat arm of the Indian Army. If it is so, then it would create parallel organisation structures in the entire gamut of command and control, communication, maintenance, training facilities for each of the Army commands. Now this thought process and the proposal needs an in depth analysis, scrutiny and I would like to take a nationalist approach in looking at these.

Unlike the independent air forces of several major nations of the present-day world, particularly in the western world, the Air Force in India has been an independent service ever since its inception some 73 years ago. The IAF is the fourth largest air force in the world today. In the early sixties in the wake of Sino-Indian border conflict, the government sanctioned a force of 45 combat squadrons for the IAF, to become a balanced air force which has not happened even till today.

Now we are talking in terms of attack helicopters, medium-lift helicopters and fixed-wing aircrafts for the army at command, corps and divisional levels. Let us pragmatise (sic) this proposal with the IAFs experience which is still struggling to become a 45 squadron Air Force.

The IAF is still pitching for acquiring some 125 multi-role combat aircrafts and if these come through, it will hopefully become a 45-squadron Air Force.

The IAF is difficult to be ignored by the world powers due to its size, combat experience and professional skills. This reputation has been acquired over the period of seventy years. Considering the level of this august audience, it is not necessary to go in to various aspects which determine the size and the force structure needed for a credible defence in qualitative and quantitative terms.

Force structuring must start with national security objectives and it is only in the Government of India, MoD Report (2002-2003) that the national security objectives of the country have been spelt out for the first time. It is virtually 55 years after our Independence that the national security objectives were laid down by the MoD. We all know that from the national security objectives flow the strategy (ies) -military, economic and so on. From military strategy, we work out military doctrines, joint doctrines and then the force structures. Thereafter, respective services carryout their own force structuring and go ahead with mission oriented planning. The mission oriented planning tells you the gaps, critical areas and the resources are accordingly allotted. We have done nothing of this kind. We have national security objectives of which many of the senior officers are not even aware of. I do not find any discussion among the three services on force structuring and mission-based planning for the armed forces.

The size and scope for the envisaged expansion of AAC in India would entail very vast outlays in defence expenditure in the next four-five plan periods. I am not hopeful that it is possible by 2017. The advanced jet trainers which were promised in 1994 are yet to come; perhaps by 2008 we would get these. The light combat aircraft (LCA) was to be in service by 2002. It is unlikely to join combat service even by 2010. These are the kind of delays and slippages, which take place in the planning process. So, merely by giving a wish list and saying that resources will not be a problem, the plans will not materialise.

What about the infrastructure in terms of runways, hangars, maintenance, repairs that would be required for the proposed AAC. And if we are to operate such a large helicopter force, who is going to provide favourable air situation for this force? Air Force would need up gradation to provide favourable air situation to Army to operate with such a large helicopter force in the combat zone. Army's own AD groups will not be sufficient for this.

Another aspect that I wish to highlight here is when Army bids for all those the areas and activities, which were the domain of the Air Force till yesterday, what will happen to the professional manpower which has been so painstakingly trained and brought up by the Air Force. Do we just dump them?

I would like to emphasise that let us think nationally and act as a united armed force to develop our abilities in a need-based manner.

It is often said that India will be a developed country by 2020, but we still have 25 per cent people living below the poverty line, 40 percent people who are illiterate and the country ranks 126 in the human development index. People still die of starvation, malnutrition and preventable diseases. Farmers commit suicide. Therefore, I think it is our duty as service officers to ensure that we provide defence capability that this country requires with the least cost that we can. That is what optimisation is all about. The rule of systems analysis says that, "sub-optimisation of sub-systems is essential for optimization of the total system." The proposal of optimising the sub-system will sub-optimise the total system. Thank you.

Lieutenant General E.A. Vas

I have just one comment to make. The aim of the seminar is to discuss Army Aviation: 2025. If after 20 years Pune is the same Pune as it is today, I have no comments to make about the seminar. But will it be the same? Twenty years would certainly bring in some changes.

Even if I was to take the pessimistic line of Air Marshal Kulkarni or the optimistic line of Lieutenant General Oberoi, I am still left with one doubt in my mind. Today the price of Oil is over $ 50 a barrel. Estimates by experts indicate that by 2010 the price will be $ 100 a barrel. Is the government going to subsidise you and me for the petrol we buy? Let us suppose, it does. But by 2025 the experts feel that there will be a steady decline in crude oil production. I think their prediction is correct as it is a finite element. What is going to be the impact of oil shortage on tank warfare and aviation? It must be taken in to account as there will be no fuel to run these machines.

We have alternate sources of energy but these cannot replace oil especially when it comes to propel military hardware. Therefore, I recommend to Director, CLAWS that whatever recommendation that we might make about the seminar, one paragraph must be added that the government must give the Armed Forces an energy statement and ways to tackle this problem in the next 25 years. How the overall energy crisis is going to be tackled and what is going to be its impact on our armed forces? Then only I suggest that you will have a sound growth plan for the AAC.

Unidentified Speaker

Sir, citing examples of resources of the past may not be very relevant for the future. To create a war fighting force, resources will have to be allocated as it was emphasised by Admiral Pasricha. Pakistani leader Z.A.Bhutto said, "We will eat grass but we will make the nuclear bomb". Pakistan made the atom bomb and they are still not eating grass.

Threats have to be realistically analysed and not in a perfunctory manner and later blame the fiasco on paucity of resources. Can India be held to ransom by repetitive episodes like Kargil and Kandhar?

We must understand that freedom of nation is paramount even above the "poverty lines". Even prosperity needs safe and secure security environment to take roots.

To my mind tardy progress of AAC is not attributable to "lack of vision" as Lieutenant General Chaki has said. It is an end result of lack of political will, impediments at decision making level, lack of understanding within and out side the Army; which is to be blamed for the present situation. Lieutenant General Mukherjee said that operating helicopters in intense environment would be difficult. I agree with him that the helicopters are vulnerable in the present day battlefield but yet these have to operate and carryout their assigned roles. Just because of threats from AD weapons the growth plan of the Army Aviation cannot be shelved. I would like to point out that a battle tank has been vulnerable in the battlefield due to anti-tank mines, missiles and other top attack munitions for years. But no one has ever suggested disbandment of the Armoured Corps. Thank you.

Vice Admiral V. Pasricha

I would like to clarify on the question of resources. I am not suggesting that the defence budget be enhanced very much from what it is today. What I reiterate is that the three services together can manage the resources better. The other point that I wish to make is that there is requirement to look at our existing manpower and infrastructure, particularly when we are thinking about technological up gradation of the Armed forces. I find that the Army is overstretched due to the

LIC and other commitments but I do believe that manpower pruning is needed if we want to usher in the RMA in the defence forces.

Major General S.G. Pitre

Sir, it has been a very exiting afternoon and a wide mosaic of views have been expressed. Air Marshal made very valid points. Permit me to elaborate on one of his points where he said that whether the whole exercise of today was for raising a tactical Air Force for the Army. If we look at 2025, probably the time has come to address this issue. The IAF is pressing for a aerospace command; so, the delineation of airspace on tactical and strategic lines is quite logical.

Speakers before me have also emphasised that the tactical airspace should be entrusted to the Army Aviation and the IAF should concentrate on the strategic arena. Command and control of such air assets which are important to fight in a TBA should be integral to the army. In this regard can we take a cue from the joint helicopter command of the UK?

Irrespective of rotary or fixed-wing aircraft the air asset which is going to be employed in a TBA should be with the Army. As far as logistics and administrative aspects are concerned, these are a matter of detail and can be sorted out keeping the interest of the organisation in mind.

Wing Commander Rathore

Sir, I am commanding a Su-30 squadron. I have an observation regarding the division of battlefield airspace in to tactical and strategic arena. It is a point of understanding as far as the employment of air power is concerned. Air power also has multiple combat arms like the Army has. The airspace cannot be demarcated in to tactical and strategic segments. Entire issue should be given a holistic view as it needs specialisation. A speaker in the previous session has said that you create AAC today and tomorrow it will breakaway (from Army) to form a separate service. There is nothing wrong if that happens as a high degree of specialisation is needed to create and run such an organisation. It is due to this fact the air forces of yore broke away from the army and became a specialist service.

Such a situation may not arise today or in the near future. What we need to address urgently is our procedures and impediments like the turf war. There is enough scope for Army Aviation and the IAF to control, grow and coexist. There is no point in carving out further niches and turfs.

The air assets cannot be divided on tactical and strategic lines. Can it be legislated that 50 kms inside the enemy territory is tactical and beyond that is strategic or up to 300 feet above the ground is tactical and beyond that is strategic? The main characteristic of the air power is its flexibility, the same aircraft which supports army's operations in the TBA also strikes at the strategic objects. So, if Army is talking about the tactical airspace then what area (s) of specialisation needs to be assigned to the AAC should also be looked in to.

Lieutenant General Amitava Mukherjee

Sir, irrespective of which agency is flying in the battlefield the requirement of AD remains; it does not matter whether it is Army or the Air Force. Hence, our AD procedures need to be sorted out.

I took part in the first exercise that was conducted for streamlining the AD procedures of Army and Air Force way back in 1980. Till today we have not been able to sort out the problem for one simple reason that the AD weapons of the Air Force are assigned a target, whereas, the AD Group (SP) is to be stopped from firing otherwise it will take on the target. Because of this dichotomy in the procedures we have not been able to sort out joint air defence centres (JADC) between the Army and the Air Force.

Basic point is the lack of inter-operability between the three services. There is no satisfactory communication between the attack helicopter and the armoured units. I think most of this can be sorted out by deliberation and cooperation. Speaking from entrenched positions is not going to help.

If the people in uniform find it difficult, the services can engage the think-tanks - the Centre for Land Warfare Studies, The National Maritime Foundation and the Centre for Air Power Studies to find a solution.

Division of airspace on the lines of tactical and strategic segment is not going to help as the trend is to go in for multi-role combat aircrafts. There are no separate aircrafts which operate in these two segments.

During the discussion you must have noticed that most of the points relate to procedures and delegation of authority. My suggestion is that let us widen the horizon of the debate and discuss about 2050, when inter-operability and digital and seamless communication will be a reality.

Lieutenant General Ashok Joshi

Sir, the discussion has been very interesting. I feel that a kind of confounded confusion prevails in the use of simple words in which we communicate our serious military matters. I would call it the lack of soft power and I tend to agree (with previous speakers) that if, the three services cannot communicate using words on which every service superimposes the same meaning, then I don't think we can get very far.

The lineage of the three services is different, the way these look at warfare is different. As far as the helicopter is concerned the Army does not think it a part of air warfare; Army uses it as an elevated platform to serve the purpose of land warfare. Air warfare has got a totally different connotation and purpose. Most of the doctrines and ideas which have been inherited by the Navy and Air Force are the ideas of island nations meant for power projection and we have borrowed these verbatim without even adjusting these to Indian conditions. This is the main problem.

Unfortunately, the Indian Army has not risen beyond the operational level. We have not gone in to the stratosphere of politico-military thinking, and perhaps that is the reason for the marginalisation of Army from decision-making process. It is a sad reality, which is apparent when you talk to any Naval or Air Force officer, he will talk about the Indian Ocean Rim countries and requirement of a blue water navy, whereas the army officers are still tethered to tactical level operations. It is a pretty serious matter. There is a need to promote strategic thinking amongst the service officers. If the services cannot put their acts together and devise a common vocabulary for communicating with each other then this logjam is going to stay.

I agree with Lieutenant General Vas that airspace cannot be divided in to strategic and tactical segments. That objective which yields you political goals is a strategic objective. Mere calling an Air Force as strategic Air Force does not give you strategic objective. So, I feel that enlightened dialogue amongst the three services will help more than equipment procurement.

Brigadier Shandil

Sir, when we cannot sort out our procedures I think it is a case of 'the tail (is) wagging the dog'. Let the services make up their mind about what is to be done and the rest is minor staff duties aspect. If for forty years we have not been able to put procedures in place for a simple thing like communication, I think in the next 20 years our efforts will remain inconclusive.

If we want the three services to operate in unison, conformity and with a common perspective, mutually acceptable procedures are important.

Airspace management is Air Force's responsibility and how it manages the airspace of the TBA it is the air force's problem. If needed, the Air Force can raise a separate agency which can set procedures for all services to comply, but we must find a definite solution to it and not be content with the stalemate that exists today.

Air Marshal Kulkarni

I would like to respond to Brigadier Shandil. You cannot look at the past and say that's what future holds for us. Let us scrutinise the defence expenditure since independence. Till 1962, it was up to 1.65 per cent of the GDP, in 1989, it was 3.8 per cent of the GDP and then it registered a decline and now it is pegged at 2.45 per cent of the GDP. I agree that the GDP is growing but so are the costs. It is difficult to have an increase in defence budget in real terms. Do we have energy security as we do not have strategic reserves? With defence expenditure remaining constant the services have to find ways and means to cut the costs and improve efficiency by adopting business process reengineering. I am not suggesting a cut on the existing defence expenditure. I am only saying that what is given to us needs to be spent in a much more efficient manner. If the expansion of the AAC is justified and operationally urgent, go ahead and acquire it. It may be of interest to the audience that no five-year plan of the defence forces has so far been approved with in the plan period itself. At times it is approved after two-three years. In one case, it was approved after the expiry of the plan period. I would quote Lieutenant General Pankaj Joshi, the first Chief of Integrated Defence Staff, "It is my firm conviction that a plan without necessary support and resources ceases to be a plan, and it becomes a wish list. Time and again many committees and studies have remarked that there is no firm commitment of resources, particularly the finance, to the defence plans. Even if the firm commitment has been made to the last rupee, at least a broad indication of the money that is likely to be available must be given. In the absence of such commitment, plan after plan, there are slippages, leading to steady depletion of the combat edge that we once enjoyed." It further goes on to say, "The other related malady is the inordinate delay in approving the defence five-year plans. Never a plan document is approved before the commencement of a plan. It is very rare that it gets approved till the middle of the second year. In absence of this the procurement is done on ad hoc basis and not on the basis of what has been planned for. One can always prepare a wish list if you know that you are not going to get the money for acquiring the things you plan on paper".

Why I am suggesting this to you is because the NDA Government had created a hedge fund of Rs 25,000 crore as the services were surrendering the unspent funds to the MoD, to the tune of 4-5,000 crore every year. This hedge fund could be utilised from time to time despite the '31st March syndrome'. However, the UPA Government abolished this fund. This is an indication of what the present government thinks. What does it show? The lack of political will to build up the defence forces. I am not suggesting that it is not likely to improve in the future. The point that I wish to make is that these are the conditions in which we are functioning. If we still feel that this kind of helicopter force is justified and the resources for it will be available, go and get it.

We must also consider the life cycle cost of these equipments. Perhaps it is easier to acquire the equipment 'off the shelf', but where would you house them? What about their maintenance? Who would fly them? What about the trained manpower? These questions would need answers not only during the initial period but during the entire life cycle of the equipment.

Is Army prepared to permanently second its helicopter pilots to AAC? If you want world-class competence it cannot be achieved in an ad hoc manner.

Therefore, the manpower, infrastructure, training facilities, etc., which the army will be required to raise, consequent to expansion of AAC will be a duplication. Whether the army should take over what air force already has or manage it jointly or raise it separately is an important question. Hence, the services should sit together and discuss it. If the service HQs find it difficult then the think-tanks of Army, Navy and Air Force which are Delhi-based can offer solutions.

It is a question of integration, jointmanship and system integration and not of unmindful expansion of a particular service. We should rather aim for having a joint plan, joint doctrine and a mission- oriented budget.

Major General B.S. Pawar

Sir, the way out which will forge integration (amongst the services) is the ALH route. It is going to be an indigenous effort except for the engine. The ALH will be a common platform on which the equipments will be fitted, all three services are keen on ALH and the HAL is the nodal agency. Induction of ALH will commanalise the training, maintenance, logistics and all other aspects. There is no denying that jointmanship is needed whether we go in for the ALH or any other helicopter. The impression is that the AAC's vision is to expand to a 300 helicopter fleet. I want to allay the apprehensions, what we are looking at ALH class utility helicopters which can carry a section-plus strength and placed at the disposal of a corps commander. The airspace management is not a problem and it can be sorted out. If it can be sorted out during exercises it can be sorted out during war. There will be fratricides, it is happening in Iraq where there is no opposition. That can be no reason for not going for expansion of AAC.

Next helicopter which the AAC is looking at is a ten-ton class helicopter which can lift a company strength, especially so in the mountains. Troop lift capability at the corps level is important and we want to buildup that capacity whether on ALH or ten-ton class helicopter.

AAC is not looking at seamless expansion. Weaponisation of ALH will address the problem of attack helicopter. The cadre management is a problem as the fleet is increasing it is becoming more acute. What we are going in for is a permanent cadre. It is slowly increasing. Recently, I came across an advertisement for naval pilots, where the Navy has gone in for short service commissioned officers. The Air Force is also opting for a similar arrangement. Army is also contemplating on having short service commissioned officers as pilots.

So the AAC is not planning for an unbridled expansion, we are planning what we are capable of handling with the infrastructure that is available.

Lieutenant General Vijay Oberoi

Why there is such a hang up about the rotary and fixed-wing aircraft. If there is a requirement we must use the platform which is most suited and there are many roles which can be better and cheaply performed by small fixed-wing aircrafts. So why deny the AAC from such aircraft.

Roles like communication flights, surveillance, aerial command post, etc. were brought out by the speakers along with their advantages and disadvantages. But suddenly hackles come up when you talk about fixed-wing. I think it is a situation of what will be effective in a particular operational requirement. If it is fixed-wing, use fixed-wing, if it is rotary-wing, use rotary-wing.

I may be giving a bad example, but take the case of the Pakistan Army Aviation (PAA). A large number of fixed-wing aircrafts are with PAA. Has the Pakistan Air Force suffered because the PAA has so many Mushaks? I don't think so. The point that I wish to make is that we are not in a zero-sum game that the advantage or gains of the AAC will be the loss of IAF.

The requirement of AAC, irrespective of the type of platform must be met. The other point is that the visualization in our mind is that when the AAC talks of fixed-wing it is referring to bombers, fighters and large transport aircrafts, etc. This is not true. The AAC's requirement of fixed-wing aircraft is modest and is of small aircrafts which can be used for a number of purposes. Another operational reality is that the Air Force has shifted focus from the ground (operations); it may be having good reasons for it. The IAF visualises that executing close support tasks in the TBA will not be possible due to preponderance of AD weapons in the battlefield. Hence, the Air Force suggests that Army should accept interdiction.

That is the view of the Air Force because they do not want to endanger their aircraft. However, the point is that close air support is still essential for Army. So, one has to find a method for managing this and not say that the Army's requirements are unreasonable or unsound.

When I was Additional Director General Perspective Planning with Late General B.C. Joshi, the then COAS, we undertook a small exercise and counted 274 landing grounds in the north-east, which could be used by these small aircrafts. These landing grounds were constructed during the World War II because of the Burma Campaign and Hump Crossing etc. We also did a feasibility study using lakes for landing. But, unfortunately you get stymied due to the lack of support and progress.

The institutional view of the IAF has been expounded today as has been done earlier also. Sadly, we seem to be prisoners of our mindset. I think we need institutional change if we want to progress. Ultimately no one can stop progress. Despite the delays and procrastination things will materialise.

I do not think that the CLAWS is there for Influencing that opinion. We do organise seminars but we do not organise these with any hidden agenda as was mentioned today by some.

Lot of speakers talked about availability of funds, I want to ask one question, can you have economic development without security? Lest we get away with the notion that we should be satisfied with the present fund allocation, I want to emphatically say that the present allocation which is around 2.5 per cent of the GDP and which has hovered there for the last 13 or 14 years is just enough for sustenance. Admiral Nadkarni had brought out that about 85 per cent of the defence budget goes in to revenue expenditure and no modernisation can really take place with this measly allocation. So at every forum we need to bring up this point instead of saying 'No'. If you want security you will have to spend money. Today the Indian Armed Forces, among all the armed forces of the world, irrespective of which denominator you take - the GDP, percentage of men in uniform, percentage of government expenditure, etc., receive the least amount of money. It is a fact. Yet we want services to deliver in war, in peace and in all conflict situations.

So, we need to be little more circumspect when we talk about this in outside fora.

Gentlemen, I am not here to create a situation where the inter-services relations get more fragmented. In fact, I have always tried for forging better relations. The reason why the turf is important is because the size of the pie (defence budget) is very small. Otherwise, if there was plenty to go around, there would be no turf wars at all. Yet, turfs are important. So, every service wants to hold on to what it has and is loath to let it go, even when the logic demands some thing else.

The future will be characterised by less wars and more conflicts. In such a scenario highly centralised organisations which are unlikely to evolve what is needed -small, compact, self-contained, mobile formations which can exploit a fleeting opportunity. Such formations and units must have integral resources, which are highly responsive. Hence, decentralisation is the key.

There is much talk of limited war primarily because of the nuclearisation of the nation, which was mentioned obliquely during the discussions. I wish to make two points. First, all our wars till date have been limited. Limited war, as a concept is not new to us. In 1947-48, the war was limited to J&K. In 1962, we did not use Air Force. In 1965, we did not touch East Pakistan. In 1971, on the western sector, we held back our Air Force for whatever reasons. In all wars with Pakistan we have deliberately not targeted the economic targets and even the Kargil conflict was localised. So, to attribute the limitedness to the nuclearisation in the region is incorrect. It is the same theory which the American and western analysts have hoisted on us and we picked it up. Pakistan was delighted on our admission to this newfound strategic reality. Secondly, the use of nuclear weapons even by countries like Pakistan in my view is most unlikely. Even if its use is visualised it will be as a last resort.

But many of us have convinced ourselves that Pakistan will use nuclear weapons as a first resort. Even for the most reckless, nuclear weapons are the last resort. We seem to have taken the rhetoric of Pakistani leadership on its face value.

Gentlemen, can a commander be denied the complete wherewithal , which he needs for fighting a successful battle? Winning is crucial and it cannot be sacrificed at the so-called 'turf'. So, if the AAC needs a particular type of aircraft, it should be given.

Manpower policy and planning of the AAC was mentioned in passing. There is a need to expand AAC so that a worthwhile permanent cadre of aviators is created and command of all associated personnel whether from the ordnance, EME or any other corps is shifted to AAC.

Lastly, I would like to reiterate that the AAC needs to grow to its legitimate size, modernise and maintain itself. It should also be restructured where necessary, and its roles and doctrinal aspects relating to its employment be redefined, so that it is fully geared up to face the challenges of the future. Thank you. ■

Some Helicopters in the Service of World Armies

SA 341/ 342 GAZELLE

Country	:	USA.
Licensor	:	Boeing.
Type	:	Day/ night, twin-engine attack helicopter.
Vintage	:	1976.
Military Utility	:	Attack helicopter.
Weights	:	Empty: 5165 Kgs. All-up: 10,422 Kgs.
Engine	:	Two General Electric T703-GE-701 C turbo-shaft engines.
Rotors	:	Four-blade foldable main rotor, four-blade tail rotor.
Crew	:	Pilot, co-pilot.
Speed	:	147 knots (323 km/h)
Range	:	228 nautical miles (501 km)
Armament	:	30 mm cannon; 16 Hellfire missile or rockets, modification (?) for Stinger/ Sidewinder/ Mistral missiles.
On-board Equipment	:	Longbow millimeter wave radar and mast-mounted rotating antenna; coloured multi-purpose display, target acquisition designation sight, pilot's night-vision sensor, FLIR, image intensification TV and missile warning system.
Fleet Size	:	Over 1,048 aircrafts (all AH-64 A and D) have been produced since 1984 till 2002. About 500 US Army AH-64D to be upgraded to Longbow configuration by 2006.
Variants	:	AH-64A, AH-64D Apache, AH-64D Apache L (Longbow).
Countries	:	AH-64D is in the service of USA, UK, UAE, Saudi Arabia, Singapore, Israel, Egypt, and Greece.

(NATO Name Hind)

Country	:	Russia.
Licensor	:	Kazan Helicopter Production Association.
Type	:	Multi-role medium helicopter.
Vintage	:	1961.
Military Utility	:	Troop and cargo carriage, search and rescue, cas evac, armed roles, direct air support, electronic warfare, airborne early warning and mine laying.
Weights	:	Empty: 15241 Kgs. All-up: 13,027 Kgs. External: 8,800 Kgs.
Engine	:	Two Klimov TV 3-117VM turbo-shaft engine.
Rotors	:	Five-blade main rotor and three-blade tail rotor.
Carriage	:	
Crew	:	Pilot, co-pilot and fight engineer (if needed).
Troops	:	24-26.
Casualties	:	Twelve stretchers.
Speed	:	113 knots (210 km/h)
Range	:	307 nautical miles (570 km)
Armament	:	The Mi-17 is provided with missiles, bombs, small arms, cannons and anti- tank/ anti-personnel mine dispenser.
On-board Equipment	:	Communication, navigation, radar, auto pilot, photography equipment, rescue hoist, IR jammers and flare dispensers.
Fleet Size	:	Over 11,000 (Mi-8) and 7,300 (Mi-17) aircrafts have been produced for civil and military use.
Variants	:	There are many variants of Mi-8/ Mi17 for civil and military usage. Latest variant is Mi-117.
Countries	:	In service of many Asian, African, European and South American armed forces. World-wide use in civilian sector.

SA 330 PUMA

Country	:	France.
Licensor	:	Eurocopter (Aerospatiale).
Type	:	All-weather, day and night, medium-sized transport helicopter.
Vintage	:	1968.
Military Utility	:	Troops and cargo transportation, search and rescue and cas evac.
Weights	:	Empty: 3615 Kgs. All-up: 7400 Kgs. External: 3,200 Kgs.
Engine	:	Two Turbomeca Turmo IVC turbo-shaft engines.
Rotors	:	Four-blade main rotor and five-blade tail rotor.
Carriage	:	
Crew	:	Pilot, co-pilot and third crew member (if needed).
Troops	:	16-20 equipped troops.
Casualties	:	Six stretchers and six seated casualties.
Speed	:	146 knots (271 km/h)
Range	:	309 nautical miles (572 km)
Armament	:	20 mm side-firing cannon and 7.62 axial machine gun; missile and rocket pods.
On-board Equipment	:	Communication, navigation, EWR-99 Radar Warning Receiver, auto pilot, landing system, map display, etc.
Fleet Size	:	697 aircrafts were produced by 1987, production has since been discontinued.
Variants	:	SA 330/ B/ C/ E/ F/ G/ H/ L/ Orchidee, Denel Oryx (South Africa) IAR-330 (Romania), Westland Mk 1 (UK).
Countries	:	Variants of SA 330 are in service of armed forces of about 40 countries, chief amongst these are Chile, France, Indonesia, Kenya, Morocco, Pakistan, Portugal, Romania, Singapore, Spain, Switzerland, UAE, UK.

KAMOV Ka-27 & Ka-28 (NATO name Helix)

Country	:	Russia.
Licensor	:	Kamov Helicopter Company.
Type	:	Naval Combat Helicopter, all-weather, day /night operation.
Vintage	:	1981.
Military Utility	:	Anti-submarine warfare and search and rescue.
Weights	:	Empty: 6062 Kgs. All-up: 12,000 Kgs.
Engine	:	Two TV3-117VMA engines.
Rotors	:	Folding three-blade co-axial main rotors, no tail rotor but triple tail fins.
Carriage	:	
Crew	:	Pilot, co-pilot or tactical coordinator and ASW system operator.
Troops	:	Up to 12 troops.
Casualties	:	One/ two stretchers or three seated casualties.
Speed	:	135 knots (250 km/h)
Range	:	108 nautical miles (200 km)
Armament	:	ASW AT-1MV torpedo (1)/ APR-2 rocket (1)/ OMAB bombs (2)/ depth charges (10)/ sonobuoys (36).
On-board Equipment	:	Communication, navigation, radar, RWR, auto pilot, dipping sonar, IR jammer, chaff/ flare dispensers.
Fleet Size	:	Over 500 aircrafts (all Helix versions) have been produced 1980-2002.
Variants	:	Ka-27PL/ PLM/ PS/ PK/ PV, Ka-28, Ka-29, Ka-32.
Countries	:	Variants of Kamov are in service of navies of Russia, CIS, China, India, Vietnam and former Yugoslavia.

CH-47D CHINOOK

Country	:	USA.
Licensor	:	Boeing.
Type	:	All-weather, day /night operation, medium-lift helicopter.
Vintage	:	1963.
Military Utility	:	Troop/ weapon/ cargo lift, Special Forces operations, cas evac and search and rescue.
Weights	:	Empty: 10636 Kgs. All-up: 33,316 Kgs. External: 12,700 kgs.
Engine	:	Two Textron Lycoming T55-L-712 turbo-shaft engines.
Rotors	:	Two three-blade, tandem-rotors.
Carriage	:	
Crew	:	Pilot, co-pilot.
Troops	:	33-44 troops.
Casualties	:	24 stretchers.
Speed	:	140 knots (259 km/h)
Range	:	325 nautical miles (600 km)
Armament	:	AAMs, window mounted machine guns, Chinook HC Mk 2 (UK) retrofitted with 7.62 mm mini-gun and infrared sights.
On-board Equipment	:	Communication, navigation, radar, auto pilot, missile warning system, ECM, FLIR, night-vision, IR jammer, chaff/ flare dispensers, rescue hoist and mid-air refueling gadget
Fleet Size	:	Over 1,160 aircrafts (all CH-47's versions) have been produced by .2002.
Variants	:	CH-47 A/ B/ C/ D/ E (Special Forces)/ F (cargo), Chinook HC Mk 2, Mk 3, HT-17 (Spain),
Countries	:	Variants of Chinook are in service of armed forces of Argentina, Australia, Egypt, Greece, Iran, Italy, Japan, South Korea, Libya, Morocco, Netherlands, Singapore, Spain, Thailand, UK, and USA.

OH-58D (KIOWA WARRIOR)

Country	:	USA.
Licensor	:	Bell.
Type	:	OH-58 (Kiowa) Light observation helicopter, OH-58D (Kiowa Warrior) Scout and attack helicopter.
Vintage	:	OH-58 (Kiowa) 1969, OH-58D (Kiowa Warrior) 1983.
Military Utility	:	Two seat scout and attack helicopter.
Weights	:	Empty: 1281 Kgs. All-up: 2495 Kgs. External: 907 Kgs.
Engine	:	One Rolls-Royce T703-AD-700 turbo-shaft engine.
Rotors	:	Four-blade foldable main rotor, twin-blade tail rotor.
Crew	:	Pilot, co-pilot/ observer.
Speed	:	120 knots (222 km/h)
Range	:	300 nautical miles (556 km)
Armament	:	Four Stinger AAMs or Hellfire ASMs or two seven-rocket pod or one .50 in machine gun.
On-board Equipment	:	RWR, IR jammer, FLIR, video recorder, real-time video downlink, SINCGRAS radio, GPS, laser warning receiver, mast-mounted sight with TV and IR optics; laser range finder and designator; airborne target handover system, digital map display.
Fleet Size	:	Over 2,270 aircrafts (all OH-58's versions) have been produced since 1962 till 2002. About 424 modified to OH-58D configuration since 1983 till 2002.
Variants	:	OH-58 (Prime Chance), OH-58D (I) Kiowa Warrior, OH-58D MPLH.
Countries	:	OH-58 is being used by Australia, Austria, Spain, Taiwan, Turkey, and USA while OH-58D's are in service of USA and Taiwan armed forces.

AH-64D APACHE

Country	:	USA.
Licensor	:	Boeing.
Type	:	Day/ night, twin-engine attack helicopter.
Vintage	:	1976.
Military Utility	:	Attack helicopter.
Weights	:	Empty: 5165 Kgs. All-up: 10,422 Kgs.
Engine	:	Two General Electric T703-GE-701 C turbo-shaft engines.
Rotors	:	Four-blade foldable main rotor, four-blade tail rotor.
Crew	:	Pilot, co-pilot.
Speed	:	147 knots (323 km/h)
Range	:	228 nautical miles (501 km)
Armament	:	30 mm cannon; 16 Hellfire missile or rockets, modification (?) for Stinger/ Sidewinder/ Mistral missiles.
On-board Equipment	:	Longbow millimeter wave radar and mast-mounted rotating antenna; coloured multi-purpose display, target acquisition designation sight, pilot's night-vision sensor, FLIR, image intensification TV and missile warning system.
Fleet Size	:	Over 1,048 aircrafts (all AH-64 A and D) have been produced since 1984 till 2002. About 500 US Army AH-64D to be upgraded to Longbow configuration by 2006.
Variants	:	AH-64A, AH-64D Apache, AH-64D Apache L (Longbow).
Countries	:	AH-64D is in the service of USA, UK, UAE, Saudi Arabia, Singapore, Israel, Egypt, and Greece.

Mi-25 (Akbar)
(NATO Name Hind)

Country	:	USSR (Russia).
Licensor	:	MIL.
Type	:	Twin-engine attack helicopter.
Vintage	:	1970.
Military Utility	:	Attack helicopter.
Weights	:	Empty: 8,570 Kgs. All-up: 11,500 Kgs. External: 2,400 kgs.
Engine	:	Two Klimov TV3-117 VMA turbo-shaft engines.
Rotors	:	Five-blade main rotor, three-blade tail rotor.
Carriage	:	
Crew	:	Pilot, weapon operator and flight engineer (if required).
Troops	:	Eight.
Casualties	:	Two stretchers and two seated causality.
Speed	:	145 knots (270 km/h)
Range	:	243 nautical miles (450 km)
Armament	:	Eight Shturm/ Ataka anti-tank missile, four Igla AAMs, two 500 kg/ four 250 kg/ eight 100 kg bombs, four S-24B rockets, a variety of machine guns fitted on pods, grenade launchers, mine dispensers, etc.
On-board Equipment	:	RWR, IR jammer, flare dispenser, gun camera, night vision, communication, navigation, auto-pilot, etc.
Fleet Size	:	Over 5,200 aircrafts have been produced since 1970. About 700 are in service of Russian Army.
Variants	:	Mi-24, 25 and 35s.
Countries	:	In the service of over 45 Asian, African and European countries.

Mi-26
(NATO Name Halo)

Country	:	USSR (Russia).
Licensor	:	MIL.
Type	:	Heavy-lift helicopter. World's largest helicopter.
Vintage	:	1977.
Military Utility	:	Troop, weapon, ammunition and cargo lift.
Weights	:	Empty: 28,259 kgs. All-up: 56,113 kgs. External: 20,040 kgs.
Engine	:	Two ZMKB Progress D-136 turbo-shaft engines.
Rotors	:	Eight-blade main rotor, five-blade tail rotor.
Carriage	:	
	Crew :	Four.
Troops	:	40 (standard) and 100 in high density mode.
Casualties	:	?????
Speed	:	159 knots (294 km/h).
Range	:	430 nautical miles (796 kms).
Armament	:	
On-board Equipment	:	
Fleet Size	:	More than 300 aircrafts built since 1977 and used as civil and military aircraft.
Variants	:	
Countries	:	

HAL 315 B Cheetah

Country	:	India
Licensor	:	License-built version of SA 315-B Lama of Aerospatiale
Type	:	General-purpose five-seater helicopter.
Vintage	:	1968.
Military Utility	:	Reconnaissance & observation and communication helicopter.
Weights	:	Empty: 995 kgs. All-up: 1,750 kgs. Under slung: 1,000 kgs.
Engine	:	One HAL built Turbomeca Artouste IIIB.
Rotors	:	Three-blade foldable main rotor and three-blade tail rotor.
Carriage	:	
Crew	:	Two.
Troops	:	Three. or
Casualties	:	One stretcher.
Speed	:	192 km/h (115 mph; 100 knots)
Range	:	260 nautical miles (500 kms).
Armament	:	Armed version (Lancer) is fitted with two 12.7 mm machine guns and two 70 mm rocket pods of three rockets each.
On-board Equipment	:	Rescue hoist, cargo sling.
Fleet Size	:	More than 250 aircrafts built by HAL till 1996.
Variants	:	SA 315B Lama.
Countries	:	India (Army and Air Force) and Namibia, Nepal.

HAL 316 B Chetak

Country	:	India
Licensor	:	License-built version of SA 316-B Alouette of Aerospatiale
Type	:	General-purpose seven-seater helicopter.
Vintage	:	1968.
Military Utility	:	Reconnaissance & observation and communication helicopter.
Weights	:	Empty: 1,230 kgs. All-up: 2,200 kgs.
Engine	:	One HAL-built Turbomeca Artouste IIIB turbo-shaft engine.
Rotors	:	Three-blade foldable main rotor and three-blade tail rotor.
Carriage:		
Crew	:	Two.
Troops	:	Five. or
Casualties:		Two stretchers and two sitting.
Speed	:	100 knots (185km/h).
Range	:	275 nautical miles (477 kms).
Armament	:	
On-board Equipment	:	Rescue hoist, cargo sling.
Fleet Size	:	More than 250 aircrafts built by HAL till 1996.
Variants	:	SA 316B Alouette.
Countries	:	India (Army, Navy, Air Force, Coast Guard), Namibia and Nepal.

Advanced Light Helicopter (ALH)

Country	:	India
Licensor	:	HAL, India.
Type	:	General-purpose helicopter.
Vintage	:	2000
Military Utility	:	Multi-role, multi-mission helicopter in 5.5 ton class.
Weights	:	Empty: 2,900 kgs. All-up: 5,000 kgs.
Engine	:	Two Turbomeca TM-333-2B turbo-shaft engines.
Rotors	:	Four main and tail rotors.
Carriage	:	
Crew	:	Two.
Troops	:	
Casualties	:	
Speed	:	135 knots (250 km/h).
Range	:	356 nautical miles (660 kms).
Armament	:	
On-board Equipment	:	
Fleet Size	:	
Variants	:	
Countries	:	India (Army, Navy, Air Force, Coast Guard).

Index

B